Loving Conversations With Me

CAROLINE PALMY

Hey,

Welcome to this wonderful book brought to you by That Guy's House Publishing.

At That Guy's House we believe in real and raw wellness books that inspire the reader from a place of authenticity and honesty.

This book has been carefully crafted by both the author and publisher so that it will bring you hope, inspiration and sensation of inner peace.

It is our hope that you thoroughly enjoy this book and pass it onto somebody who may also be in need of a glimpse into their own magnificence.

Have a wonderful day.

Love,

Sean Patrick

That Guy.

www.ThatGuysHouse.com

I dedicate this book to me:

The girl I was

The woman I am now

And the woman I am growing into more
and more each day

I dedicate this book to all of you who are
on your path, growing into the loving
person you are meant to be.

♥

FOREWORD

Love is a force more formidable than any other. It is invisible—it cannot be seen or measured; yet it is powerful enough to transform you in a moment, and offer you more joy than any material possession could.

Barbara de Angelis

Love yourself first and everything else falls into line. You really have to love yourself to get anything done in this world.

Lucille Ball

When I think of Caroline Palmy, I picture her warm, vivacious smile; her open, kind heart; and her ability to love unconditionally. She sees people as they truly are—a unique Presence of the Divine. What I know is that LOVE is her natural way of being. She reminds us that everyone has the capacity and ability to love and to be loved.

In *Loving Conversations With Me*, Caroline shares her clarity and discovery about loving. It's through her willingness to FEEL the human emotions of hurt, anger, sadness, shame, betrayal, and unworthiness that love has the potentiality to emerge, revealing strength, power, and the infinite possibilities of life itself. She lets us know the necessity of healing old patterns, false beliefs, and ways of being that no longer serve us. Caroline shares her travels to freedom as she births this Presence of love, no longer limiting herself and walking in lockstep with what the world thinks of her. She declares, "Accepting myself, feeling worthy, and feeling loved were the steps I needed to take so that I could heal all past relationships and patterns." Most significantly she writes, "Self-love is embracing all of yourself—not just the good parts—but everything: every cell in your body, every thought in your mind. It's about seeing yourself as a whole and loving yourself completely."

Many books have been written relative to the magnificence of being a loving Presence. Caroline brings to our attention what is possible as she consistently and consciously does the work necessary to be liberated. "The work—loving, even when it's hard to love." As Caroline writes, "I learned to fill my cup first and let it overflow—and only after I felt filled up, I then shared with all my heart."

Allow this book to remind you of the importance of practicing unconditional self-love so that you not only practice loving yourself, you get to practice loving EVERYONE—especially now.

Blessings and love,

Karen Mills-Alston, ALSP

Author of the book series,
10 Principles for a Life Worth Living

CONTENTS

INTRODUCTION

Welcome to *Loving Conversations With Me*.

I am sharing insights into self-love, self-worth, and love, itself—insights I realized when I was going through the situations I'm recalling in the book, and sometimes while looking back, working on healing. The stories from my life might inspire you to open up to more love in your life and for yourself every day.

I share the stories as I remember them; sometimes I've shortened them or edited them to make my point clearer.

My aim is to spread love to the world and help you, my gorgeous reader, to open your heart to the love that's there for you, too.

As I am sharing from my life, I'm using different names for others to keep some privacy for my loved ones and the people who used to be close.

The people in these stories are:

I am myself, Caroline. Yes, this is my name, and I have nothing to hide— not from myself, not from you, not from the world.

Mathew is my gorgeous first-born son.

Catherine is my amazing daughter.

Horatio is my wonderful youngest son.

Toni is my ex-husband.

Jane is Toni's new wife.

James is my past boyfriend and rebound lover.

Jason is James' son.

Enjoy this book. Enjoy the stories and dive into the *Wisdom From The Heart* assignments.

I hope this book helps you to learn more about love and all the matters of the heart. I'd love to enlighten the world, one heart at a time. I hope I can bring some light and love to yours.

♥

DESPERATELY LOOKING FOR LOVE

Do we tend to look for love in all the wrong places?

Oh yes, definitely. I did so many times, myself. I see now how I was desperate for love, and I did things I am not proud of. I can understand why these things happened when I look back with loving eyes. There are things in my past I was too ashamed to share, things no one knows about me. I have a lot of empathy for the Caroline I was 20 plus years ago. She felt so lonely— so deeply unloved—she was desperate to find love.

I feel many of us are looking for love. Some people might search for love and validation in things, thinking, "When I have this car or that house, then I will finally be someone, then people will love or adore me."

Yes, there are also people like my ex-husband, Toni, who confuse adoration with love, or who might not be looking for love at all, but for something different like feeling worthy or being seen as someone who is important.

Others might pursue a demanding career, need to be constantly in motion, or hoard material objects in their homes.

All of these quests are similar though. Deep down, we are all looking for the one thing I call LOVE.

Some people can't stand the emptiness. They'd rather drown their feelings—or the lack of feeling loved—by eating or drinking or taking other substances just to numb their pain, their emptiness, their failure in finding love.

Personally, I did drink more when I was married and as a young adult. I was feeling so low, I thought I needed to drink, and I even got drunk on a couple of occasions. Toni was not pleased, to say the least. Maybe my drinking was the little part of me that wanted to rebel against him, that tiny part that still asked me to stand up to him. Of course, once I was pregnant and had kids, I did not drink much. Later, towards the end of my marriage, there were evenings when Toni and I had two bottles of wine between us, so that was a lot. Yes, I drowned my sorrows back then. I drowned my voice, and alcohol gave me that fuzzy warm feeling, a little bit like love, and for a tiny moment, I could feel *love*.

Of course, I know nowadays that getting drunk is not the way to connect to love. I understand why I drank and why others do it, and I send love and healing to that part in me and that time in my life. Sharing compassion with yourself and your past is important.

I love children; I always wanted four, as I have two sisters, and with the three of us, it felt it was always two against one. I did not like that at all. My sisters shared a room and had a cord as a line in the middle, splitting their sides. I was only allowed to be on the side with the sister I aligned with. It was bloody awful, so I wanted four kids so that there would never be two against one. Now I know there might have been three against one, if I'd had four children.

Now I have three wonderful children, and it feels less like two against one, as it is a different combination. They are not all girls, and, unlike my two sisters who are identical twins, I had three single births. Boy. Girl. Boy.

Still, I wanted more children. Deep down, I wanted lots of children. I always LOVED being pregnant. I always loved to cuddle up with my kids, and I felt it was the greatest feeling on earth to have children. Number four never happened for us though, and for a long time I mourned the fact and felt broody.

One day a friend told me that I should think about what was behind my wish to have more and more kids. What was lacking in my life?

Back then, of course, I was furious with her. I wondered how she would dare say such a mean thing to me. She had no idea what it felt like to hold a newborn, to feel that love and bonding and that eternal bliss. Kids are wonderful, and they are a gift—I felt that I knew that better than she did.

Only later did I realize that wanting to have more kids was actually a sign that I wanted to feel more of that love—the pure joy and love—I felt for my children, and the love they gave back. Yes, I realized I was needy for affection and I was trying to fill that void with children. At that time, I didn't realize that love could come from me—I was always looking for love outside of myself, be it through my children or my romantic partners.

There are also people who confuse sex with love, and yes, I am guilty of that, too. I had affairs. Yes, the liaisons happened when I was married to Toni, before we had kids. It was at the time when I realized my marriage was empty, and I was not receiving the love I craved from my husband. It was a time when I felt deeply unloved—extremely unhappy—and a time when I needed to get validation from other men that I was lovable.

This is my deepest and darkest secret, something I felt ashamed of, and something no one knew about. Even though I fully understand where this behavior came from, it still feels like some sort of a failure to me. I was not strong enough to keep up my marriage vows. I failed; I was not good enough. These types of beliefs and thoughts were the feelings that drove me toward other men, plus the lack of sexual satisfaction with my ex-husband. In a way, it was also a test to see whether I was functioning properly, as I never experienced orgasms with my ex-husband. I was intensely lonely in my marriage until I had kids; the children helped me feel more emotionally fulfilled.

When I was together with James, the man I dated after my divorce, the first thing he mentioned was that his ex-wife had several affairs, and how detestable he thought that was. He came from a strict Catholic background, and it was the gravest sin in his eyes to have an affair. So from the start, that relationship was not based on truth, as I could never share with him that I was no better than his ex. He put me on a high pedestal and told me that he knew I would never have an affair. Of course,

I did not have affairs while I was with James, as we had a fulfilling sex life. Deep down, though, I felt guilty and was ashamed of myself in some ways. I felt deeply regretful and had to hide a part of who I was, which only caused me not like myself very much.

Nowadays I can look back and embrace that young woman who felt so profoundly alone, lost, and unloved, who felt she had to try and find love with other men. It never worked; it never would have. Sex was not the answer and not the path to love either.

Those affairs were something I did back then and something I felt was the way towards LOVE. I no longer feel ashamed. I no longer feel sorry. I have filled that void with a love that is stronger than anything, with the only true love there is—the love from within, the all-encompassing love of deep understanding and compassion for myself. Now I can look myself in the eye in the mirror and tell myself, "I love you, Caroline," something I could never have done back then.

I have a deep trust that I am worthy of love—that I am love.

You know, we all come from love, we all go back to love, and we all try to connect with that all-encompassing love in any form we think might lead us to it.

Where are you looking for love in your life?

What past version of yourself can you send some compassion to?

Wisdom From The Heart

Take a minute to breathe deeply, down into your belly.

Close your eyes. Let your thoughts wander to a moment of shame in your life.

Breathe into that moment. Maybe you even feel a little shame when you think about it now.

Now shine some light onto it. Let the sun go up on that time. Let the sun shine onto you back then, warming you, clearing your energy, and loving you.

Feel into yourself. What was going on in you back then?

What were you running away from? What were you running towards?

What was lacking in your life back then?

Feel into the moment and let yourself feel compassion for your past self. Sense where you were coming from. Send yourself some love.

Hug yourself. Imagine you are hugging yourself from now to yourself from that time. Tell your past self that everything will work out just fine. Tell her you understand her. Send her love, compassion, and understanding.

Sit with her for as long as you need.

When you are ready, come back into the here and now. Move or shake your body. Tune into how you feel in the present and how you now feel about your past.

You can do this exercise with anything from your past you are not proud of. It is deeply healing and clearing and will allow you to embrace ALL of you.

If we hide or resent things from our past, we can never fully accept ourselves as we are.

Heal your past and set yourself free. You are so worth it.

FAMILY REUNION

Was there a time you felt like you were accepted just the way you were?

Oh yes! There was one distinct day when I saw the light at the end of the long grey tunnel. It felt so good to feel accepted, to know I did not have to pretend like I was someone else. It was so liberating just to be *Caroline*, and know deep down that my uncles and aunts knew me—they've known me since my birth—and that they accepted me just the way I was.

It was a chilly November day when I, for the first time in over 20 years, attended a family reunion.

My mother had nine siblings, and I have over 30 cousins. We saw each other often all through childhood and a bit during our teenage years.

I remember I felt a bit intimidated and a bit tepid before going to this family reunion. I hadn't seen my mother's family for quite a long time. I wondered:

Will they still accept me?

Will they still remember me?

Will they be angry that I never made it to any of the reunions?

Was I an outsider again?

Would I ever fit in?

You know, I had good excuses for not attending reunions in the years before that. We lived abroad or far away. It felt like too much hassle to travel with three young children. Also, my ex-husband was not too keen on family gatherings, so I never attended any.

After my relationships with Toni and James ended, I was ready to come back into the circle of my family.

My three children were a bit overwhelmed by the reunion, as they never got to know our big family because they hadn't been introduced.

I remember entering the place and seeing some familiar faces, seeing the smiles on my aunts and uncles faces when they saw me. It was wonderful; it felt like a big homecoming. I felt safe and relieved, and I knew that, yes, this was where I belonged.

Feeling the hugs and kisses returned me to my childhood. I thought, "Yes, this is what family is all about."

They welcomed me with open arms. They were all so happy to see me, and it felt so tremendously good to be wanted and loved.

Even though it had been over 20 years since I last saw some of my relatives, it felt to me like I had just seen them, like I had only left a day before and was back from a short journey. My mom had done an excellent job, too, telling me about births, marriages, and other changes to the family.

I realized I could breathe again. It was a new way of deep breathing into my core, it seemed. I felt the expansion, the connections, and the love.

I was home, after nearly 30 years of walking my own path, searching the world, wandering around, feeling so alone and unloved. I was back. I realized that I had so many amazing aunts and uncles who knew me since I was born, and they loved me just the way I was.

I did not have to pretend any longer; I did not have to please them; they knew me, some even knew me better than I knew myself.

They accepted me, too. I felt a huge relief wash over me, like being a child again and being showered in understanding, love, and empathy.

Yes, they acknowledged where I was coming from as well. Some of them had experienced the same or similar—divorce, lost love, being away from family for an extended period—and here I was, the lost child, the prodigal niece, the long-lost Caroline.

It was such an amazing experience, being accepted for who I was, who I am. There was no need for small talk or to worry about what I said. There was no need to fear that I did not look good enough, or that I did not fit in.

This was the first time in a long time that I could just be me.

I did not need to explain myself, I could simply be. Wow, that was like an entirely new experience to me. How refreshing and odd it felt all at the same time.

I remember sitting with my cousins and catching up, remembering how we were best friends in childhood. We still felt that connection, feeling the same sense of understanding and mutual respect.

Here we were, all around 30 to 50 years old—grown adults—and still feeling like the children we had been.

I spent the afternoon exchanging memories, reconnecting, laughing and simply being myself. It was liberating and felt so loving.

Seeing myself through the eyes of my family, feeling the love they felt for me—just me, not a pretend version of myself—helped me relax.

Yes, I am loved.

Yes, I am lovable.

Yes, I am enough.

I breathed this in and cherished the moments even long afterward, which helped me allow myself to be, to learn to accept myself just the way I was, and yes, it helped me remember that I am lovable just the way I am.

In the arms of my aunts and uncles, I did not need to do anything; I did not need to work hard to be loved. They simply loved me. Wow! It was an amazing realization.

I remember shedding tears of relief, and it felt so good. I was still timid and fragile, but I finally felt a little better. I knew that if they loved me just for being me, that I was lovable, and that I could learn to love myself too, just me, Caroline, just the way I was born to be. All I needed was to remember that I am part of this amazing family.

That was the turning point for me. It was the day I realized I was acceptable and I did not have to do anything to be accepted. All I really needed to do was to be myself, and that was enough.

Have you ever felt truly accepted?

Wisdom From The Heart

Accepting yourself can be tricky. I know it took me nearly 50 years to do so.

Was there a person in your childhood you felt close to, a person—maybe a favorite aunt or uncle—who you felt accepted you and loved you for who you were?

Or do you have a distinct memory of a moment when you felt accepted and loved?

Take some calming breaths.

Close your eyes and reconnect with this person who accepted you or the moment when you felt acceptance.

Sit with it. Feel into it. Expand the feeling. Reconnect with the acceptance and love you felt. What were you doing in that moment? How did it feel?

Feel into it deeply, reconnect, and breathe the feeling into your heart. Expand your heart with the feeling of love, breathing it in more and more. Fill yourself up with that feeling of love and acceptance.

Breathe. Feel it. Let it fill you up. And then sit with it.

When you are ready, come back into the here and now.

Reconnect with the feeling of love and acceptance as often as you need. Fill up your being with love when you feel low or when you doubt your worthiness. Focusing on times when you felt cherished and will help you to recognize the fact that you are loved and accepted just for being you.

We all are worthy of love and acceptance. You are no exception.

I am love.

You are love.

We are all love.

CORNERS VERSUS THROW-INS

Is love always fair?

Yes, love itself is always fair; however, sometimes we overdue it in the name of love.

For example, as parents, we have to ask ourselves the question, "What is love?" Is love letting your child do as he/she likes? Is it giving in every time a child has a tantrum or gets upset?

How do love and fairness come into perspective for a parent?

As a mom of three, I had to deal with fairness and love all the time. There wasn't one day when one or the other of my children told me, "That is not fair!" or "You love him more than me!"

Parents who have only one child might have an even tougher time bringing fairness into love. Children who have no siblings to share with might enjoy undivided attention from both parents.

Again here, do we let our children win all the time, or do we sometimes let our children lose, too? Do we share life—real life—with our children? Is life all about winning all the time, or is it also about taking turns, waiting, and learning to be part of a wider community?

I am no child expert, and I know there are a wide variety of answers to all the questions above and people who support all different ideas.

So, we get back to the question: How can love be fair? For example, for me, as a mom of three, it seems like no one gets enough attention and I have to divide my love all of the time—but is that the worst thing? It's kind of like nutrition: we don't have to have a well-balanced meal all the time; however, over the course of a day or a week or a month, we aim to maintain a well-balanced diet overall. This is the same with children. We can't give same amount or quality of attention to all of our children during every minute, but it does balance out when we look back at it over the months or years.

Yes, I had to explain to each one of mine that I, of course, pay more attention to the one who needs me most at a time. When one is sick or hurt, I tend to that child more and over time it balances out, as they were all sick or hurt and had their time for my undivided attention.

Love is endless. I feel like my kids always feared that when I gave one more love, then there was less for them. However, I knew all along that love multiplies; it doesn't split with each child. It's not that we love our firstborn any less when the second one comes along, is it?

So love is always fair. It's only when we, as parents, feel the need to intervene that it becomes unfair, like the following story might demonstrate.

James loved to play soccer. Horatio was thrilled, as he also loved to play soccer. James' son, Jason, was about the same age as Horatio. There were afternoons when they all played soccer out in the garden: James, Mathew, Catherine, Horatio, and Jason. It didn't always end well, or we can say it didn't end well often. You see, Jason was an only child and James was a bit overindulgent with him, allowing Jason to ignore rules they had made for the game if it suited him. As much as I understood him wanting to have a special relationship with his son, I didn't feel he taught his son well by coddling him.

Somehow, they made the agreement that Horatio would always do the throw-ins and Jason would always do the corners for this particular soccer game, however there were many more throw-ins than corners, so Jason got upset and started to throw a tantrum.

My three knew they would not get away with tantrums, and were likely more used to sticking with commitments.

So James—wanting to keep his son happy and avoid tantrums—just took the ball away from Horatio and said his son would be doing the throw-ins. Had he only asked Horatio, or offered him a corner next time, all would have been well, however Horatio, of course, started to complain because it was not fair. How could it be when an adult just snaps away the ball and starts changing the rules mid-play, just because Jason was complaining. There is always a way, if we only try and talk.

I agreed with Horatio—and not just because he's is my son. If James had explained to Horatio and asked him to alternate or switch off, it would have been different. Or really, if he had done anything to negotiate a more fair way of doing things, it would have been different. Horatio is a beautiful sensitive child, and would have loved to hand over the ball to Jason, if he'd only been asked.

When you have more than one child, you become skilled negotiator. I am a skilled negotiator of peace. It didn't seem to me like James had any experience with negotiating at all.

So all of a sudden, everyone had a say in this game and tempers flew high.

Jason was not happy and threw a huge fit, destroying things in the garden. I've never seen a six-year-old throw such a tantrum, just because the world did not revolve around him.

James was not happy and blamed Horatio, so Horatio came running towards me, screaming, "This is not fair! We had an agreement!"

Everything was too much for me. So I stood and told James to take his son and go for a walk to calm him down or do something to create some distance and allow everybody to cool down.

Of course, James got angry with me on top of it all.

Discussing it later had no impact, as according to James, everyone else was at fault. James wanted to make his son happy and was above any understanding of anyone else's feelings or needs.

There were many more times like this when I was with James. He also manipulated my children into doing things his son wanted. These weren't my best moments, because I saw what was going on but tried not to interfere. I did not step up for my children. I was more inclined to try to make James happy.

James seemed to fear that his son would not love him if he didn't constantly make him happy.

I feel deeply for children and parents who don't see each other often. I know how tempting it might be to spoil those children, as we want to shower them in love and maybe make up for the time we've missed. However, by spoiling them, we aren't doing them any favors.

Loving them fully is a different matter—yes, and love itself can never spoil a child. It is our perception of what love is that might end up doing more harm than good. If we allow children to eat chocolate all the time or give them whatever they want when they demand it, it is not a sign of love.

Enjoying time together, sitting with each other, hugging, and yes, serving healthy nutritious meals, being fair, teaching them to honour agreements, and being a wonderful example is what love is all about. As a parent, those are the loving gestures.

Being there for them emotionally, holding them, and listening to them is much more valuable than always giving into their tantrums. Allowing them to feel their feelings, showing them how to sit with their feelings, and teaching them that life goes on is love.

Life is not always fair; however, love always is. Trying to take all of a child's pain away and keep him happy isn't doing him any favors; on the contrary, this is a huge disadvantage for a child. How will he ever be able to cope with disappointment in his life if we are always bending over backwards to make his life happy?

Yes, Horatio still talks about that UNFAIR soccer game. He had an advantage though: he had two older siblings so he knew he had to play fair, and he knew that he couldn't always get his way. He also understood that life isn't about being happy and having your way; life is about playing soccer and having fun.

I hope James and his son have found a way back to normalcy and a way to learn from each other.

Love is always fair. It might not feel like it in the moment, but love is always fair.

Does it feel fair to love yourself?

Wisdom From The Heart

Do you feel self-love is a good practice, or do you feel you might be selfish if you put yourself first sometimes? Do you feel guilty or feel that, if you love yourself, you might be taking away from others?

Do you feel you should love everyone and everything else first, before you can even start loving yourself? Do you feel like you are worthy of love?

Or maybe you fear you are doing something bad if you love yourself.

Releasing fear, guilt, and worry is an essential part of a healthy self-love routine.

Here is how you can start to release those negative feelings about self-love:

Sit somewhere quietly.

Take a deep breath into your belly and release it with an open mouth (you are encouraged to sigh or make a sound).

Ask the Angels to assist you.

Ask Archangel Michael to cut all energy cords with his mighty sword.

Keep breathing, as you imagine Archangel Michael cutting through all the cords around you.

Now take another deep breath into your belly.

Ask Archangel Michael to cut all the cords to fear.

Breathe into your solar plexus (below your ribcage)

Fill this area with beautiful yellow light.

Say, "I am." *(So ham)*

Ask Archangel Michael to cut all the cords to worries.

Breathe into your solar plexus.

Fill this area with more beautiful yellow light again.

"I am."

Ask Archangel Michael to cut all the cords to guilt.

Breathe into your solar plexus.

Expand your solar plexus.

Breathe in deeper and deeper.

And say:

"I AM Worthy.

I am worthy.

I am worthy."

Breathe in deep.

Breathe out and let it all go.

Thank Archangel Michael for his assistance.

Feel into your solar plexus.

Put your hands there and breathe into your hands.

Give thanks.

Come back to the here and now and open your eyes.

I love to call on the Angels for help. Archangel Michael's energy is amazing.

Do this exercise daily or more often if you need to.

The more you do this exercise, the more easily and quickly it will go.

Remember, clearing your energy field is like taking a shower—you need it daily.

♥

NO ONE LOVES ME

Was there a moment you felt deeply unloved?

To be honest, when I look back, I don't think I ever felt truly loved. I felt I needed to be a nice girl or like I had to be perfect so someone could love me. The moment my relationship with James came to an end was the moment I felt more unloved than I ever had before—so utterly out of love—that I told myself no one loves me.

This was also the turning point of my experiences with love.

James was just the opposite of my ex-husband, and our relationship felt so good. I was so in love. James truly loved me, and he understood me—at least that's what I thought. It was exciting to have a new relationship. It felt wonderful to have a completely different experience; however, it was also not right. I again tried hard to make a man happy, and while I saw he still had issues with his ex-wife and their child, and I tried to be understanding at the beginning of our love affair. After nearly two years, though, it got to be very tiring.

He tended to cancel dates the last minute, which bothered me, and I just had a nagging feeling that something was just not right. Finally, it all fell apart. I was not able to hold it all together any longer or to pretend it was a perfect relationship.

James and I had been sending emails back and forth. We hadn't seen each other in a while, and I was very dissatisfied with the situation. I remember I was blaming him for the rift, and the emails got more unloving as they continued on.

I decided to take myself out of the ridiculous blame game we were playing, and I wrote him an honest letter via snail mail. I opened up and shared my feelings from the "I" perspective (sharing sentences in the I form: I feel, I understand, I sense, etc.). I shared with him that I did understand at the beginning that he had to sort things out with his ex-wife and child, but after two years, I expected that he would be done sorting things out, and that would have stopped letting his ex interfere in our life and manipulate him constantly. It was a very honest letter, and deep down, I hoped that he would say, "Yes, please stay with me." However, his reply was, "Thank you for your letter. I do understand. Let's be friends."

This was the moment of truth. It was the end of my new relationship. James did not want me anymore. "No one loves me," I told myself. "I am not likeable. I am not nice enough. I am unlovable. No one wants to stay with me."

This was the moment when I honestly felt deeply unloved.

I lay on my bed, crying and crying. It was the first time I allowed myself to shed tears over our relationship. I was so good at holding it all together. This break up was the drop that made my barrel overflow, truly.

Actually, the barrel burst and everything came flooding out.

I remember I barely managed to drive my kids to school and came back home just to end up in bed again, duvet over my head, crying and crying till I had to get out of bed and pick the kids up again. It took about five days of letting go and crying it all out for me to hit rock bottom.

It was not just the break up with James that I was mourning. It was also the break up with Toni, which I never truly grieved, either. It was the combination of everything, all together, along with the burden of going through a divorce and having to stand up for myself and defend myself from then on. (You can read more about this in my first book *Conversations With Me*.)

It was time to let go.

After five days of mourning the end of all of my previous romances, I was ready to face the world again. I realized that I only ever felt loved when I was in a relationship. So my break up with James meant the end of love for me. It felt equal to being declared unlovable.

I remember sitting on my bed and thinking, "Wow I am needy. I am desperate for LOVE from others." I realized how I held on to my relationships way past their expiration dates—well past the end of their healthiness—just because I needed to feel loved, to feel like I was worthy of love. I needed that outside approval, that outside source of affection to feel loved.

"Wow," I thought, "I am needy and clingy." I felt sorry for the men I'd had relationships with. I was demanding love from them—and reassurance and everything. No wonder they left me. How could they ever supply all the love that I craved? How could they ever fill up the drained and probably leaky tank of love I carried around within myself?

Yes, this was the moment I felt that I was deeply and utterly alone. I was so desperate to feel loved.

This was also the beginning of a beautiful journey to reconnect with the love within myself, to remembering that we are all love.

I knew I was done being with the wrong type of man. I was done having to rely on a man to provide me with the feeling of love any longer.

I knew that I was not genuinely lovable if I despised myself so much. If not even I could love myself, how could someone else truly love me?

How could anyone see me for who I was when I was always hiding from myself?

I also felt deeply betrayed, betrayed by the trust I had in James, betrayed by LOVE. I felt he had used me, and I was angry with myself for letting him use me for such a long time. He never contributed to rent or any cost of living while he lived in my home.

I felt like I fell for a con artist. I wondered whether any words he uttered ever contained any truth, or whether he was just such a great salesperson.

I realized I let it all happen to me because I so desperately wanted to be in a relationship. How pathetic was I?

So this was truly one of my lowest points. It was also a point of no return.

I swore to myself that I would never ever be with a salesperson again.

AND I would never ever be so NEEDY of love that I let myself be used.

I vowed to find love through other means than men.

I had no idea how I was going to do that, but I knew I would figure it out.

So I began learning more about spirituality, getting connected to the Universe, the Angels, and I learnt to connect with myself—to connect with Caroline, who she truly was.

And a gorgeous journey to love began.

This journey to reconnecting to the love within myself was starting: a profoundly compassionate, deeply understanding, deeply accepting and profoundly loving journey.

When was the last time you let go of your sorrows?

When was the last time you allowed your tears to flow?

Wisdom From The Heart

If I am ever in a stressful situation or feel a bit out of sync, it helps me to shake it all off.

Imagine yourself being a polar bear or a dog.

Stand on all fours—kneel on the floor and put your hands down as well.

And then shake, shake, and shake and stretch your body out.

You can also do this standing on your feet—shake or dance wildly while releasing the energy trapped within you.

Imagine that everything is just flying off you. Then stand still and feel within yourself.

Pay attention to what you feel. Does it feel any lighter yet, or do you need to shake more?

Once you feel like everything has been released, you can continue with your day, and remember to shake it all off whenever you need to.

♥

DOUBLE WHAMMY

Do you feel that people need time to get over a relationship?

Absolutely. Quite frankly, when I met James in May after my marriage of nearly 20 years ended only four months before, I was not truly ready yet.

I hadn't had time to grieve the loss of my marriage. Yes, it was grief—the pain of a broken relationship. Going through a divorce is sometimes even worse than losing a loved one to the Universe, as we know our exes might be living happily with other partners while we are left alone, hurt, and sad.

It is OK to resent our ex-partners for a while, or even to hope they are having a hard time. We go through the stages of grief—one of which is anger.

We should allow ourselves time to heal from a past relationship.

How long does it take to heal? I have no idea. It depends on the person, the situation, and probably how the relationship ended.

I truly feel it takes time to heal and get over a relationship, and the healing comes in phases.

We might have friends who step from one relationship into the next, just to experience the same issues over and over again. I think of those situations as the same guy in different colors: first in blue, then the same in red, and then the same in green. Experts call it a *relationship pattern.* It just means that we are looking for the same experience in a relationship, working through the same issues, even though we are not aware of it. We might be expecting the next guy to be better than the previous one, only to realize that he is the same kind of person again.

This cycle shows the need to heal the pattern within ourselves, so we can choose a different kind of partner.

Also, some try to escape the pain and hurt of a break-up or bad relationship by starting a new relationship, only to later realize they have not fully mourned the last relationship, and then carrying the baggage or unfinished sadness with them into a new relationship, which is often called a rebound relationship.

I had my rebound relationship with James; actually, we were both on the rebound from broken marriages. I expected him to be my final one, THE soul mate I had been waiting for all my life. I pinned too much hope on one guy and settled back into unhealthy patterns, allowing myself to live to please him, to do anything to make it work, instead of walking away when I probably should have. I was so desperate for him to be The One.

Yes, healing from a past relationship is essential before we move on to the next. I could only put the energy into healing when I was single. I could finally grieve my broken marriage and mourn my broken relationship with James once I was by myself.

I ended up with a double whammy to deal with. I probably needed the sledgehammer, one-two punch to come to my senses and finally take the time to heal, let go, and mourn.

I had the opportunity to look for love within myself instead of only feeling loved when I was in a relationship.

Being single helped me to connect to my own truth again. I learned to feel worthy and loved just by being me.

When was the last time you truly felt loved or worthy, just for being you?

I am not recommending that we dump our partners or we need to be single to connect to our own love and worthiness. This was the way I needed to do things; however, there are many other ways to connect with our own truth. I know of people who are happy in their new relationships, without having gone through extended healing processes. They might have healed already during their former relationship.

As a girl, I always felt I needed to be the nice girl, do the right things to feel loved—to even really be worthy of love.

So being nice became my thing. I did what I thought others would approve of so that I could feel like I deserved to be loved.

It felt completely alien to be worthy of love by simply being myself. It couldn't be true. Didn't I need to be better or do something kind in order to be loved?

Accepting myself, feeling worthy, and feeling loved were the steps I needed to take so that I could heal all past relationships and patterns.

I needed to learn to be ME, to figure out what I liked, instead of adjusting my tastes to please the men in my life. That's why the Universe kept me single, so I had time to become myself and to love who I was. Otherwise, I would have been too busy loving my partner, instead of loving myself.

So yes, if you are going through this yourself, give yourself enough time to heal from a break-up, mourn what no longer is, distance yourself from romance for a bit, and allow yourself to feel angry, sad, guilty, happy— whatever comes up. You are grieving; it's normal. Allow yourself time to heal. Give yourself as long as it takes, and don't think another romance might be the trick to get over your pain. It rarely is.

And sometimes, years later, another layer of grief comes up or one you thought you had dealt with appears out of nowhere. That is normal and it means that you are just healing on a new level again, over and over.

Allow healing to take place and embrace the pain, whenever it comes up.

When was the last time you allowed yourself actually to sit with your feelings?

Wisdom From The Heart

Sit comfortably.

Breathe deeply into your belly.

Close your eyes.

Ask for Mother Mary to come forward and help you heal your heart.

Imagine Mother Mary sitting in front of you, facing you.

She is holding her hands over your heart, and she asks you to breathe out the pain you feel into her hands.

Breathe in and breathe out of your heart.

Breathe out all the pain and hurt into Mother Mary's hands.

Allow the tears to come up—crying is releasing.

Keep breathing in and breathing out the pain and hurt for as long as you need.

When you feel like you are done, thank Mother Mary.

Come back to the here and now.

Open your eyes.

You can do this exercise anytime you need. I still use it on occasion for my own healing journey. Mother Mary is such a gentle and gorgeous heart healer.

♥

NOW YOU KNOW WHAT YOU DON'T WANT

Was there a moment you gained insight into how you looked at relationships?

There was one moment—I remember it vividly—when I understood that I could choose what I wanted in a relationship, that I have a say in things. It felt so strange, so weird, so out of this world.

I met my first boyfriend when I was about 14. Yes, I was young (seeing it from a mom's perspective now). I had never noticed this boy. Our relationship didn't start because I was interested in him. I usually had a crush on a boy, and then nothing happened. This time, it was the other way around. I noticed how he was interested in me, and then I sort of got interested in him. Looking back now, I know that this was not love. This was just falling for it, or confusing love. He was into me, and I was flattered. Yes, it was amazing; there was finally a boy who seemed to like me... wow. SO I thought I had better grab him before he reconsidered.

Fear of missing out on love has been the underlying theme throughout all my relationships. There were not that many, only three so far.

I felt I needed to hold on to love while I had it. If I let go, there would never ever anyone else who would love me. I thought, "If not him, then no one." This attitude is what we might call a 'lack mentality' nowadays.

Indeed, how could I ever think there was only one man who could be interested in me in the whole wide world? I did so because I felt unloved, because I felt incomplete, because I felt unworthy. So I used to settle for the wrong men all the time, because I would rather be with the wrong man, than be alone. Being alone meant failure, that meant no one liked me, no one thought I was worthy. Being single seemed like a failure back then. Nowadays, I am happily single, and my saying is more like, "Rather single, than with the wrong man."

So much has shifted in the last eight years since I broke up with James.

I had no idea of self-worth or self-love back then. For me, worth was always something I needed to acquire from the outside.

I only felt loved when I was in a relationship, so how could I give that up? If a relationship ended, I was outside of love, and I did not want to be out of love. I wanted to feel loved, so I stayed in loveless and often unhealthy relationships far too long.

When I was out of my relationship with James, one of my aunts told me:

"Now at least you know what you don't want."

I was stunned. I thought to myself, "What? Did I have a say?" James and I met because he saw me in a coffee shop, and he was attracted to me. Again, a man I would barely notice and who was so not my type. I jumped in because he seemed to love me. He assured me that I was lovable. And I held on to that hope and feeling that he was The One for too long. Never, in my wildest dreams, had it occurred to me that I could say NO.

Why would I refuse a relationship? We know that beggars can't be choosers, and I was most definitely a beggar, a beggar for love.

So thinking over what my aunt told me, I felt the message was profound indeed. There were many things about James that did not feel right. I was embarrassed to be with him around my friends. He was too loud, too obnoxious for my taste, and on an intellectual level, we had nothing in common. The sex was great compared to what I had with Toni (nothing). After a while, though, it did not feel so great anymore.

Nowadays, I think if it is not truly a soul connection, it won't work.

Also, all the bad parts distracted us. And quite frankly, as great as it felt to have an orgasm with James— something my ex never cared about—I knew deep down there could be more. I was missing that deep connection, that heart-to-heart bond my soul was yearning for.

Again, though, I would have never voiced this. I was happy to have what I had and tried to be content with my lot.

So, thinking back and connecting with the wisdom shared by my aunt, I felt it was correct. I didn't want a man who had unfinished business with his ex, and I most definitely did NOT want a salesperson anymore.

I understood that I'd rather have an honest and humble man, someone trustworthy and educated who also speaks English and is warm at heart. I long for a heart-to-heart relationship. I'd had an intellectual relationship with my ex-husband, Toni; a sexual relationship with James; and later I had a brief long-distance relationship, which I would probably rate as spiritual. So I had it all in different forms. After my aunt told me that one bit of advice, I knew I could ask for everything I wanted in the form of *one* man, a Heart, Body, Mind, Soul, and Spirit connection.

I know he is out there, and that is OK—when the time is ready, we will meet.

Actually, there are probably many men out there who fit my wishes and would make great partners for me.

When I knew what I no longer wanted, I felt much better.

My aunt uttering this wisdom opened my eyes to something much more profound for me: I, myself, can choose, and I have a say in what I want and will accept in a relationship. I can voice what is acceptable and what not. Plus, it gave me the freedom to step away from a relationship that wasn't right for me, which was something that never occurred to me before.

This works not only for relationships but also for every aspect of our lives, from work to family and friends.

Yes, I have a say, YOU also have a say in your life, and *we all* have a say in our lives.

We are able to choose what is it we know we don't want in our lives anymore.

I feel by knowing what we don't want, we are able to understand what we do want. We get more clarity, and we not only learn we have a say in our lives; we also learn something about self-worth. We are worthy of saying no, and we are worthy of choosing if we want something or not.

And one thing I learned along my path was:

BE PICKY!

Yes, we have the right to choose the best cherries and to enjoy them. They are so much sweeter and tastier than the others. So pick the best options, in all areas of your life.

You are worthy of the best, of what it is you truly desire in your heart and soul.

Do you know what you don't want?

Wisdom From The Heart

Do you ever dare to dream big?

I never allowed myself to play big or dream big. I felt I had to be content with what I had, and I felt it could be worse. So I thought I should be happy with what I had, and I kept myself small.

Here is an exercise for you:

Sit somewhere quietly. Breathe into your belly. Close your eyes.

Just sit, breathe, and relax.

Put your hands on your heart and ask your heart...

- What would I do when EVERYthing and ANYthing is possible?
- Where would I be?
- What would I do?
- How would I feel?
- With whom would I be?
- What would my day look like?

Keep breathing into these questions, feeling into them. Take a moment to expand your dreams and get a sense of who you could be if you allowed yourself to fully live your dreams.

Breathe it all in, into every cell of your body

Feel the expansion, the flow, the love.

Breathe it in,

And when you are ready, come back to the here and now.

You are allowed to dream big. If you needed permission, then there it is.

You can do this exercise every day, and you will realize how your dreams will grow and your horizon will expand, how you can expand more and more. You will learn to breathe in the possibility of it all. Over time, you will gather the inkling of the fact that your dream is becoming your reality, that you are capable of a lot more than you might have thought, and life is wonderful.

Anything and everything is possible for me, for you, and for everyone.

Keep on dreaming big. You so deserve it.

WHAT IF...? IF ONLY...

Where there times you second-guessed yourself?

Ha, ha! Are you kidding? I was the queen of second-guessing myself.

I always felt everything was my fault. If something did not work out, it was surely because of something I'd done. If people were rude or denigrating, I thought I deserved it.

Every time a relationship ended, I second-guessed myself.

I would ask myself questions like: What if I had been more patient? Could I have been more understanding? What if I had tried a bit harder?

If only I could have been more compassionate, more perfect, more adaptable.

It could have worked out, I convinced myself, if I only tried one more time.

This habit of taking the blame for everything probably started in my childhood. You see, my father was a highly sensitive person; however, back in the day, men had to be tough. They needed steady work, and though my father was an amazing artist, wonderful figure skater, beautiful violin player, and a writer (I still have some of his stories and notebooks), he worked in an office job that was too harsh for his sensitive, artistic nature. He did everything he knew how to support his family, and yes, along the way, he let go of his dreams. The only way he knew how to deal with all of this was to drink. A couple of years ago, I wrote a beautiful blog post about it all: (*No Matter How Hard I Tried,) I Could Not Save My Father.* You can find it on my website (PalmyHealing.com)

Even as a young child, I thought that if I could be a better daughter, then my dad would stop drinking. What if I hadn't said this or that? Would he feel better? Would he not drink?

Later in my childhood, when I learned that I was the reason my parents had to marry, I was burdened with more guilt. What if I hadn't come along? Would they both be happier if they found someone else?

What if I hadn't been born? What if I was never conceived? Would my parents be happier?

Those were deep musings that only furthered my beliefs of being unwanted in this world. I felt my father resented me for coming along and I often felt deeply unloved, until a day not many years ago when I saw a picture of him holding me as a little child. I saw the love in his eyes. He did love me after all. That realization brought a deep relief into my heart and a new understanding of love.

Later I wondered, what if I had stayed with my first boyfriend. We were together for half a year when we were 14, and then three years later, he wanted to get back together again. I said yes, just because—as I mentioned earlier in the book—I felt being with a man was better than being single. Though our relationship was not love—I know that now—I hoped to rekindle what we'd had years before, yet it never happened.

Then I met Toni, the man I later married, and I left my first boyfriend for him. Years later, I still felt ashamed and guilty of hurting my first boyfriend. I asked myself "What if...?" And told myself, "If only...." These degrading questions erase the last bit of self-worth a person might possess.

Now I know we were not meant to be together, and I was only with him because he asked, not because I wanted to be. It was not right for me, and not at all for him, either. He deserved a woman who was with him because she loved him and wanted to be with him. I know he is happily married and has children now. I am happy for him, and I know he understands now why it didn't work out.

I hope our families understand, too. There were years of shame and blame after our relationship. I was shamed and blamed for leaving him for another man. How could I? It was not only this fact, but I'd had a little fling with a classmate, too. Again, this fling was a sign of me reaching for—screaming for—love. That classmate was a man I felt attracted to, but of course, our affair was forbidden.

And what did I learn from these experiences? I learned that every time I reached for love, it turned sour. I learned that trying to find love was shameful; it was guilt. For years, I did not attend any class reunions because I felt so ashamed and guilty about my past affairs, until I learned that hiding and shying away is never a good solution.

I learned to look at myself with compassionate eyes, feel into my reasons, and unburden myself from societal or religious dictation. There is nothing shameful about trying to find love. There was nothing I needed to blame myself for on my journey to that love. I can accept who I was back then, sense the truth, feel compassion for my actions, and learn to let go of any shame or guilt I felt about my past. I was like a little child trying desperately to feel love.

Later, when Toni left, I felt like I deserved it. Yes, deep down, I was to blame, I thought. I did things wrong. I pushed him away. I was guilty of killing every little hope he had within him, in my opinion.

Yes, to be honest, during the last years of my marriage, I was so down and burned out, I thought my life would be easier if he died. I admit it, and yes, I felt immensely guilty for even thinking such thoughts, even though I saw it as my only way out. Little did I know that the Universe had a very different path ahead for me, a deeply healing path, a path that brought up so much that needed to be healed within me.

I share the stories about how I learnt to reconnect with myself after I woke up not truly knowing who I was anymore in my first book *Conversations With Me*.

So when James left, I sat there again, asking myself those questions once again. What if I had been more patient? What if I had tried a little bit harder? If only I could have been more compassionate toward him, and so on. I felt so lonely—so deeply alone, unwanted, unloved—that I felt, if I tried a little harder, it would all work out splendidly, and our relationship would stand the test of time.

Little did I know at the time that we were not meant to be together. I didn't fully understand that he was only there to help me over the hardship of going through a divorce. It was not even a season, only a reason for him to be in my life. I didn't understand that ours was not a healthy relationship, either. I fell for the sweet talk of a salesman; I believed every word he said and took everything he said at face value—and was sorely disappointed and hurt when I found out the truth behind his lies.

So always asking myself what I could have done better and *what if* did not help the situation or my self-worth. It kept me from seeing the truth.

It took me a while to fully see all of this and to understand that, by telling myself if I only tried harder or was a better partner, I was actually creating a pattern of people pleasing in myself. My thoughts of not being good enough fed my insecurities, and somehow affirmed that something was essentially wrong with me, and that I desperately needed to change.

There is nothing wrong with any of us. There is nothing we need to change and there is no other person in the world we need to please, other than ourselves. Anything else is unhealthy. Trust me. I know; I have been there. I bent over backwards most of my life, and it leads to burn out, depression, and a deeply dark and lonely space.

You are worth so much more, and yes, you are lovable and deeply loved.

By the way, my gorgeous friend and fellow author Elizabeth Goddard is writing a book with the title: *What if, if only.* It will be published in the not too distant future, keep an eye out on ThatGuysHouse.com .

Do you sometimes wonder what if...?

Wisdom From The Heart

Let's twist those questions around a bit. Read them out loud with me:

What if I am worthy?

What if I am lovable?

What if I am perfect, just the way I am?

What if I am the person I am meant to be?

If only I saw myself as the beautiful soul I truly am.

If only I could see myself through the eyes of others.

If only I could see the love that resides within me.

If only I was aware of how courageous and lovable I am.

If only I could see the perfection in my imperfections.

If only I could just be myself and that would be enough.

Keep repeating these phrases and questions and listen to the answers that come up for you from within.

Maybe you can find some more *what ifs* and *if onlys* on your own.

This way the *what ifs* and *if only* questions help us, instead of wearing us down.

ALWAYS THE LAST ONE

Did you ever feel like you were the least important person or the person everyone thought of last?

Oh, yes. I thought that often, and others treated me that way, too.

I know there may be some of us who still remember how hard it was to be picked for a team in gym class, and they were usually the last ones chosen.

I never had that problem in school, though. I was quite good in physical education, so I was picked early. I always felt a bit bad for the ones last on the list, though.

Think about the last child in a cafeteria food line, wondering whether there would be something left when it got to be his turn, or pondering the alternative if her first choice was sold out.

When I was married, I made sure I looked after my husband. Oh yes, he had been working; he needed downtime; dinner had to be ready; and, of course, he was the man of the house.

With James too, I naturally made him a priority in my life. I planned according to his schedule. I was always flexible. "What if he decides to come by," I thought. "I'd better keep my diary free for him just in case."

I know you might call me pathetic. How often did I pass on meeting friends, and how often did I forget to live MY life just because he might come over?

After he moved in with me, I would have dinner ready, and he would call to cancel right before he was supposed to be home.

Again later, when I moved and he had rented his own flat closer to his office, he'd also call last minute to cancel plans with me. Yes, I was disappointed and annoyed.

Then, one summer break when he was at his parents for five full weeks and hardly got in contact, I realized that I was nowhere on his priority list.

There was his son—of course, children are a priority and I fully understand that, as mine are too.

There were his parents. They were elderly and lived far away, so I sort of understood them being a priority.

There was his job. Of course, that was important

Then there was his ex-wife. I had a hard time seeing her as a priority, though.

Plus there were his friends, his colleagues, and, and, and…. And it seemed I was quite far down on his priority list, if I was on it at all.

I felt taken for granted, like someone he would stop by and see if he pleased, and someone he could cancel on with very little notice if something better came up.

I gathered all my courage and talked with James about it. I shared with him how his behavior made me feel, and that maybe having fixed days—like Tuesday and Thursday—to see each other might help. He agreed and I was happy; however, our arrangement didn't last long. Yet again, I got a phone call from him at 6 pm, telling me he wouldn't be able to make it to dinner.

I was so disappointed. I had bought extra meat for him, as I counted him in for dinner, and I felt like another opportunity was lost between us.

I realized I was waiting in line, waiting around for him to show up again. It was at a really bad point in my life—I was waiting for someone to show up, and feeling like I didn't have any other real priorities. Of course, I had the kids and looked after them, but I am more of a homebody. As an Empath, I had a select few friends—not tons of friends to go pubbing with, as others might do. I was mostly content with being on my own at the time, but I felt it would be nice to actually see my boyfriend.

I also clearly saw that, as I was often home anyway, it was easy for James to feel like he could come and go as he pleased—or perhaps NOT come at all. In his eyes, there was hardly any difference if we saw each other; in my eyes, it was like day or night.

Even weekends seemed to fall away. When we planned a weekend for us, his ex would demand he saw his son that weekend, or she would cancel visitation with his son when he was supposed to see him.

How could I be disappointed when he dropped our weekend date so he could see his son? I am a compassionate woman, and I love my kids, so I tried to understand, because I would do anything for my kids, too.

However, after a lot of interference from his ex-wife, I was truly done. I saw him as the *Hampelmann*, or the guy dancing to his ex-wife's wishes, that he was.

I felt we should be at a better place after two years together, and I had a surge of self-worth coming up. I realized I was worth so much more than the breadcrumbs he left.

I deserved more of a boyfriend than one who slept and recharged all weekend when he was with me. I wanted a man who was alive and fit and happy to see me. Even though I love to snuggle up and lie in a bit, I also wanted to do something together, and not have to drag a tired man around. I wanted quality time. Yes, he was often even too tired for lovemaking. So what was left? Nothing. Me being the nurse restoring him for the week ahead so he could attend to his priority list—the one I was not even on, you know.

Looking at it realistically, seeing what it all came down to, I realized, how little priority I gave myself. How little I valued my time and myself.

I was always available, and I tried to please him. I did everything to make it work and dropped my plans in order to have a moment with an exhausted man who didn't seem to even care.

That's when I started to stand up again, when I looked deep within myself and heard my inner voice say, "Enough is enough."

I did not comply anymore. I stopped pleading for him to come around, and the very next time he called to inform me that his ex wanted him to take his son the coming weekend again, instead of spending the weekend with me, I told him over the phone, "I didn't expect anything to be different, and I'm finished waiting around for you."

I knew I was done with our relationship. I was done being last on anybody's list. I was done with only being someone when everybody else was taken care of. I was done with James.

AND I was done with being taken for granted. I knew he was just mirroring me. He put me last on his priority list because I put myself last on my own priority list.

I knew I had to change something within myself. I had to learn to make myself a priority.

Even though I was standing in that place of empowerment, I had no idea where to start making changes.

Little did I know that I had already started it by saying NO. I said no to coming in last.

Knowing that we no longer accept being put last on the list is a wonderful starting point to making ourselves a priority in our lives.

In what area(s) of your life are you not making yourself a priority?

Wisdom From The Heart

Take a piece of paper and a pen.

Now please write down the names of the five most important people in your life.

1, 2, 3... GO!

Got it? Do you have the names of all five written down?

Look at your list, going over each name.

Is your name on the list?

Where is your name?

What position are you in?

Maybe you're like me when I did this exercise—you did not even mention yourself.

I had no idea I could put my name down on my list of priorities.

And, just like my list showed, I wasn't a priority in my life.

Now take a new sheet of paper. Write down the name of the five most important people in your life...

Including yourself.

Where on the list are you? Are you at the bottom?

Try again.

Here's a hint: You are *the most important person* in your life. I know it might feel icky, but write a new list...

With YOUR name on the top!

And treat yourself like you are the most important person in your life, because you are.

♥

VALENTINE'S DAY

Is Valentine's Day important to you?

I love Valentine's Day, and celebrating it is somewhat important to me.

When I was younger, I felt this was the day I was shown that I was truly loved. Later, I felt like a failure being single on Valentine's Day, and nowadays I learnt to celebrate Valentine's Day just for me.

I love celebrating love, and I always enjoyed dressing the kids in red for Valentine's Day when we lived in the States. They had such cute little dresses for girls, and also socks and hair ribbons with hearts. I loved that they celebrated this day at school and exchanged Valentine's cards.

It is important to show love all of the time, though, not just on Valentine's Day. I tell my kids that I love them daily, and they tell me they love me, too. It is heartfelt, and we enjoy it, and we hug each other on a daily basis as well.

There are many ways we can show the important people in our lives our love. We should do it daily, and also for ourselves.

So now, back to Valentine's Day. I remember when I was a girl, my father complained the florists invented

Valentine's Day so they could sell some flowers in February, a month when business was slow. Even though he said that, I always felt Valentine's Day was something special.

With my ex-husband, I tried to find Valentine's gifts to give him other than flowers or chocolate, as he also felt that Valentine's Day was just a good sales trick. We went to a concert once, but it was always me taking the initiative to organize something special for us to do, and after a while, Valentine's Day was just like any other day—dull and a struggle to get through.

Then with James, I was in love, and he talked about how romantic he was. I got some romantic presents for him for Valentine's Day and gave them to him before he left my home—he usually spent the week of Valentine's Day with his son at his parents' home, which was a long drive away. The first time around, I hoped we could celebrate together, but I understood that he had plans with his son. When I gave him his present, he was a bit abashed and said he planned something and would give it to me after he got back. He never gave me a gift that year.

I so wanted for James to show me he truly loved me by giving me the perfect romantic gift. I felt if he would only celebrate Valentine's Day with me, if he made an effort for once, I would know deep down that I was lovable. So when I went skiing with my kids and he was with his son, I hoped he would come by and surprise me. It never happened. It did not happen the first year we were together and not the second year, either, and we never had a third Valentine's Day.

Looking back, I realize how needy I had been, how much hope I put into this one day. I honor the woman who would have loved to celebrate love, though. I understand where her heart was at the time.

Looking back, I see that I realized deep down that James did not truly love me. I was more of a convenience for him—not a desire—and that drove my need for him to show me his love with grand gestures.

I am laughing as I write this. Yes, some people celebrate one day—Valentine's Day—with big gestures and then there is nothing else all year, so that's probably not what I was looking for either.

Valentine's Day is just a reminder for us to celebrate LOVE; to recognize love, to be grateful for all the love in us and around us, and not only on February 14th, but also on every day of the year.

It is also about showing kindness and not taking partners, family, and friends for granted. It's a bit like Mother's Day.

After James and I broke up, I felt deeply lonely when Valentine's Day came around, so I started the tradition of buying flowers for myself. I can be my own best Valentine.

Each year now, I celebrate MY LOVE for myself on Valentine's Day—self-love, and of course, my love for my children. I usually buy them some chocolate hearts too.

It got easier over time, and each year I realized I became more proud of myself and more loving towards myself, and I really learned to celebrate being single, as being single has helped me become more myself than any partnership would have ever done. Being single is not a failure; it is an opportunity.

What gift would you give yourself to celebrate Valentine's Day?

Wisdom From The Heart

We can celebrate love every day. I make a habit of asking myself what I need throughout the day, each and every day.

Put your hands on your heart.

Take a deep breath.

Close your eyes.

And then ask yourself:

"What do I need?"

Listen for the answers. They might come in the form of an inner voice, words, a feeling or sense, or maybe in the form of a picture or movie, or by simply knowing.

Keep breathing, and allow the answer to come.

"What do I need right now?"

When you know, go and do that for yourself.

The love you give to yourself will spread through your life and even multiply as it goes.

SELF-LOVE

Why is self-love important?

Self-love... What is it and why is it important? Those are such wonderful questions.

You see, for most of my life, I felt that self-love was selfish, arrogant, and borderline narcissistic. "Yeah, right. Who needs self-love?" I wondered. "Only the people who deem themselves important need it. I'd rather look after others and share my love. That's what life is all about, right?"

I felt self-love was a bad thing. Love for oneself was, in my opinion, a very selfish thought and I could never consider it.

Altruistic love was much closer to my heart than self-love could ever be.

You see, though, not filling up my own jar, not looking after myself, and especially not feeling loving towards myself only made me exhausted and unkind—the opposite of loving.

By withholding the love from myself, I withheld my love from the world, too.

By shorting myself, I shorted the world.

I realized that no matter how much I tried to share and spread love to the world, as long as I did not include myself in all the love I was sharing, it was never going to be good enough; it was not complete.

Everything changed the minute I allowed myself to love myself, and a new abundance of love started showing up in my life.

The more I loved myself, the more I was able to share and spread the love with others, too.

Let's get back to the question. Self-love is very important, because you need to feel love to be able to share it, because we—like everybody else—crave love, because if we cannot love ourselves, we are unable to truly love anyone else, and because if we are withholding our own love, we will eventually feel exhausted and resentful.

I always considered myself a very loving person. I had no idea that I wasn't as loving as I thought! I felt giving love was the best thing ever. Being loving is wonderful, and it is an essential aspect of my personality, especially as a mom. However, feeling the love and being the love by truly tapping into the true essence of our being—LOVE—is amazing. It's something different than just giving love.

As you know from previous chapters, I was looking outside of myself for love. Once I started to look inwards and connect with the love within myself, I connected with my heart, which beat for me and pumped blood lovingly through my body—just for me.

I can hardly describe what a difference connecting with the love inside myself has made in my life. Truly acknowledging myself for who I was gave me such a wonderful feeling of peace, belonging, acceptance, and love. It had been something I only dreamed about, and never realized could be part of my life. The feeling was bigger than I imagined it could be.

Like so many changes we make, my full acceptance and love for who I was did not happen overnight; however, with one step at a time, it blossomed. It was like exploring life anew, like walking through magnificent scenery and enjoying the wonders all around.

And the more I accepted and loved myself, the more I was able to share the love.

I realized that I loved my kids on a whole new level.

I also learnt that I accepted everything and everyone around me with a newfound understanding. That realization brought peace and love to me on a whole new level. I learnt love and compassion for each individual I interacted with, and also to accept my children just the way they were.

I tended to live through my children at the time—through their successes and my pride in them. Yes, like all good meaning parents, I hoped for the best for my kids. I was aware that I sometimes hoped they would fulfill my dreams, or rather that I could fulfill my dreams through them. But I learnt that they are their own people and I am just guiding them along for a short time. They are not here for me; I am not here for them either. Of course, this doesn't mean that we shouldn't take care of our kids—we absolutely should—but our children are not our life's purpose, and they are not here to make our lives feel more fulfilled. They have their own plans.

The more I allowed my children to be themselves, the more I could allow myself to be me, too. It worked the other way around as well—the more I was myself, the more I could let my children be themselves.

I learned through them. When my kids said no, it helped me learn to say no.

Recently, I nearly canceled a healing trip I had scheduled because my youngest, Horatio, had something planned for that week, too. I felt I needed to be there to help him pack his things and to send him on his way.

I went deep inside and asked myself what I wished to do. I truly wanted to go to that event, and yes, I felt guilty as a mom, though I knew he would be OK—probably even better off without me nagging him and supervising his packing. He is 15, after all. I also realized that no one was asking me to cancel my plans or step back from my wishes. They never had.

My teenagers taught me well. They did what they wanted to do, met friends on weekends, and went around their lives seemingly without a care in the world. I saw them being independent, and it allowed me to become independent.

I had to learn to step out of my mother role and to become more *Caroline* again.

By pursuing my interests without hurting anyone, I allowed others to pursue their interests, too. The more

I allowed myself to focus on what I enjoyed doing, the happier I became, the more fulfilled my life was, and yes, I felt less resentful.

Honestly, when I looked back, I realized I had been a tad bit resentful. Yes, I felt I was doing so much for others, and no one was doing anything for me. I felt like my kids were taking me for granted.

So by allowing ourselves to look after ourselves, giving ourselves permission to do the things we love to do, and allowing others to do what they'd like to do as well, we are leading more loving lives. Plus, we end up being amazing role models for our children—especially for our daughters who might become people-pleasers or look outside themselves for love as many women do. It's a win-win situation for everyone involved. It sure was for my children and me, plus my friends and family.

Where could you be more accepting of yourself?

Wisdom From The Heart

Hug yourself. Yes, I've found that hugging myself can be such a profound experience.

So, learn to hug yourself. Really lean into your arms and feel the love and acceptance radiate from within you.

Now switch your arms around; the arm that was on top now goes under the other.

Oh, this is less comfortable, isn't it?

So hug all the parts of you: the parts you love, the parts you do not like that much, the parts you like to hide from yourself and others, and even the parts of yourself you don't truly like. Hug yourself some more. Feel into it, and say:

"I love you, (your name), fully. I love all of you, (your name)."

Keep doing this wonderful exercise. It will lead you to accepting all of yourself and to more self-love. And remember, self-love isn't selfish at all.

DATE NIGHT

Is it hard to do things by yourself?

I have to smile at this question. Yes, hammering in nails or lifting heavy stuff is not always easy. I am really grateful I have two boys who help me with 'guy things.'

Also, going on a date just by myself was equally hard, at least until I got used to it—then I actually enjoyed it!

When James called me to cancel yet another weekend, and I knew I was done with our relationship, with him and everything that went with him, I still had a dinner reservation at a restaurant for us. I wanted to cancel, but a little voice in me asked *why?*

Yes, I felt silly going out for dinner by myself, sitting at a table all alone, looking at all the couples and families around me.

Then again, I had the reservations. My kids were with a babysitter, and I was truly looking forward to the lovely food.

So I went out alone—a date night by myself. It felt a bit weird because it was the very first time I had dined out alone. I took a book along so I could read, as I had no one to talk to.

Yes, I felt that people looked at me a bit funny, but they didn't bother me.

Of course, I was also a bit sad about the breakdown of my relationship with James. I still hoped that he would come to his senses and realize what he was missing out on.

I had a glass of wine with my dinner; I was still able to drive home after only having one drink with my meal.

I enjoyed gorgeous food, too. And do you know what? I ate more slowly, and somehow I savored the food more. There was no distraction because I was on my own.

I felt everything during that dinner. I felt alone, abandoned, left out, and weird, but I also enjoyed that time just by myself.

There was no one to ask me questions, no one to have a conversation with but me. There weren't any awkward situations, either.

I was at peace in peace all by myself.

I honestly felt this was the proper way to dine. I remembered movies of grande dames dining on their own while staying in hotels by themselves.

It felt good in a way, too. I had a new appreciation for my newfound strength. I celebrated who I was by going out by myself.

Going out felt much better than sitting at home alone. I did not have to cook. I could eat wonderful food, have a beautiful glass of wine, and simply enjoy the experience—enjoy life.

However weird it felt at first, I soon realized this was an amazing way to dine, and I promised myself that I would go out for dinner by myself more often.

I could enjoy a date night by myself, celebrating me.

Why not?

Have you ever been on a date by yourself?

I also used to go to the spa alone on the weekend when there were a lot of couples. This felt awkward though, as there were a lot of conversations going on—but I actually wanted to have some quiet time. Of course, I missed James even more then, being the single one among the couples.

Generally, if I go to the spa by myself, I prefer to go during the week and enjoy the peace and quiet because it isn't so crowded. I usually take a notebook with me, because I have the greatest insights and ideas when I am relaxing in the spa. I take many notes in between my sauna sessions. It is a fantastic experience, and I love it.

I can highly recommend a spa day by yourself. Go when there are not that many people, and you will enjoy it even more.

A friend of mine loves to go to the theater; however, she does not want to go on her own. I asked her why she doesn't.

How often do we wait until we have a partner to do the things we long to do? Then once we have a partner, he might not be into the same things we are—so we might have waited for nothing or to drag a frustrated and bored partner with us.

After my break up with James, I vowed not to wait around for another partner to do the things I wanted to do. I promised myself I'd do them when I wanted and by myself.

I am happy to go to the theater by myself. I love hiking, and I especially love doing it by myself—OK, my dog usually comes along, and sometimes Mathew joins me. I stopped waiting for the perfect day to hike or for a day when Mathew has time, too. I go when I feel like it, company or no company.

I plan my sauna and steam bath days by myself and during the week because I love them for my health and relaxation.

I value my time more, so I have become choosier about whom I spent time with. That also makes the time I spend by myself feel like it's more quality time. More quality time means a happier life for me.

If I want to watch a movie in the cinema, I go and watch it by myself, and yes, if I'm craving some good food, I might just take myself on a date.

What is the one thing you always wanted to do, but never found the right person to do it with? What is stopping you from doing it by yourself? You are so worthy of the time and experience—enjoy the things you love to do, and don't wait around for the perfect friend, partner, or time. Do it now. Enjoy YOUR life.

Don't waste your life away waiting for a better time.
Now is YOUR time.

*When was the last time you had a date night just for
and by yourself?*

Wisdom From The Heart

Do you have a bucket list?

A bucket list is a list of things you'd love to do, and a list of places you'd love to visit.

If you don't have one, it's no problem. If you do, it's always good to update it.

So take a piece of paper and a pen.

Sit down and put on some soothing music.

Take some deep breaths.

Close your eyes.

Then ask yourself:

What places would I love to visit?

What cities?

What countries?

What kinds of places would I like to explore (mountains, beaches…)?

What are things I would love to try?

What are things I loved to do as a child?

What was the one dream I had as a child?

What were the places I wanted to go and visit as a child?

What would I do if I had all the money and time in the world? (Allow yourself to dream big on your bucket list)

Take time to note it all down.

Let it sit for a while,

And then go over this list every now and then again.

Like the Dalai Lama said, visit a new place each year. Maybe you can make plans for this year or the following year—a little day trip or a weekend getaway. Do something that you'd LOVE to do each year, and each day and every day. You are so worth it.

MAY

Is the month of May special to you?

Oh, May is the month of love, in my opinion. It's a beautiful spring month (here in the northern hemisphere) when everything is in bloom, gorgeous colors are everywhere, birds are chirping, everything is awakening, and yes, there are many romantic weddings.

I met James in May. I took it as a sign that we were truly meant to be together. I felt it was a sign from the Universe that he was the one I'd been waiting on for so long.

Glorious May, indeed. I love spring and May is always a favorite month for me. Even as a girl, I dreamed about my wedding, with a horse-drawn carriage, beautiful dress, flowers, and yes, the man of my dreams declaring in front of everyone that he would be with me for all of time.

Even though I am a true romantic, I did not get married to my ex-husband in May; we married in November instead. November is an excellent month to head out to the sun in the Caribbean for your honeymoon.

Back then, I had already realized Toni wasn't perfect—but then who is, right? Despite some nagging doubts, I went ahead with the wedding, as planning the wedding was wonderfully fun, and I hoped that everything would be better once we were married. I ignored the fact that our sex life wasn't filled with fireworks, but I thought sex would be less important later in our marriage and he was the man I felt I could have children with. He was older and more secure, and he was the means to my dream of becoming a mom coming true, as he was able to support my dream.

So I entered my marriage with a naïve dream of things getting better, but they never did. Of course, I was afraid of speaking up and communicating my wishes. I let imperfections and misunderstandings slide by and I adapted to the discomfort.

Did I have the wedding of my dreams? No. Weddings cost a lot of money, so we made the most out of what we had. Yes, we had a lovely dinner, and I am happy my father was still alive and was able to walk me down the isle.

Did I have the marriage of my dreams? No, not really. Yes, I had three wonderful children with my ex-husband, but it wasn't a happy marriage or a partnership.

With James, I hoped that all my dreams would come true and that I would finally have it all—everything I always dreamed of. I was grateful to have a second chance at romance and was so head over heels, that I didn't speak up or communicate my needs and thoughts once again. I was still too timid. I did what I did best; I adapted.

And I probably held on for far too long, because I met James in May and felt it was a sign of undying love. Yes, I switched things around to make excuses for him and his behavior.

Deep down, I always hoped James would rescue me. I wished that everything would be simply wonderful with him. Yes, I was still naïve, even though I was a bit older.

Looking back, I feel compassion for myself—maybe naïve is not the right word to describe what I was at the time. I was—and am—a girl with dreams.

Having dreams is wonderful. It brings cheer to our lives, and also gives us a sense of purpose, showing us where we want to go. Acknowledging our dreams and following up on them gives us direction in life. Dreams show us what we truly wish for. So we shouldn't discard our dreams, they are road signs for the direction we want to go in life.

However, each one of us is the one who needs to follow through with our own dreams, taking steps towards making our dreams come true on our own. We can't wait around for someone to rescue us, for a knight in shining armor to come and grab us, swing us onto his horse, and carry us off towards our dreams.

You see, I never realized that I was the creator of my own life. I was the only one responsible for my happiness. I always handed that part off to others, to the men in my life. I hoped they would take me in their arms and carry me to my dreams.

Unfortunately, it didn't merely end in heartbreak and disappointment, but also in internal immobility; giving my power over to the men in my life rendered me lame and powerless.

While I met James in May, it wasn't a sign for me to bend over backwards to make it work. No, it was simply a sign that he was there for me during a time when I needed him, and likewise, I was there for him when he needed me. Nothing more, nothing less; it was just that. Our experience together was OK, and I am grateful for the time we had together and for the dreams that I allowed to wake up within me again.

May is the month of blooming flowers, and I started to bloom again when I was with James.

For a long time, I did not want to marry again. I figured I had done that, it was a big disappointment, and I never wanted to experience the same frustration again. I never wanted to give up my independence—a feeling I had worked so hard for—ever again.

I lost trust in the institution of marriage.

Nowadays though, I feel that I am ready again—ready to try to find my own way to celebrate romantic love. My new dream does not necessarily involve horse-drawn carriages or churches. I don't know exactly what it is; however, I know I am open to getting married again, which is a wonderful achievement in itself. So I am entering MAY in my life again.

You might laugh to find out that my ex-husband married his new wife in May. Yes, he married for the third time

(I was his second wife) in May. And yes, back then I was a bit miffed. Now I feel happy for him and happy it is not me he married this time around.

What dream did you give up on?

(Was there ever a dream you gave up on because you felt silly or thought it wasn't possible?)

Wisdom From The Heart

Time to dream.

As a young girl, I loved to daydream; yes, during my teenage years I spent a lot of time fantasizing about boys.

I later gave up on those daydreams, as they never seemed to come true.

Nowadays, I know it is essential to tap into my dreams.

I allow myself to dream big, and I connect with my dreams on a daily basis.

I also keep my dreams open. For example, I don't dream about a specific man, but rather about a man who has the characteristics I am looking for.

If I dream of this book becoming a bestseller, I see myself signing books or speaking about this book.

I feel into my dreams. I try to experience my dream as if it is already true.

I also ask what I need to do to make my dreams come true. I ask for guidance from my Higher Self, the Universe, and the Angels.

Do you love to tap into your dreams?

I love Mike Dooley's books, especially, *Infinite Possibilities*, and his e-courses, like *The Matrix*. He is also the author of the wonderful TUT notes, daily dose of inspiration.

It is so essential to keep your dreams positive and wide open. When you do so, you don't have to worry about the HOW's. You just let the Universe and your desires guide the way.

♥

I WAS ALWAYS A GIVER

Giving is a beautiful way of sharing. Do you think you can over give?

Oh, most definitely! I was an OVER giver most of my life. It led me to suffer from burnout and depression for a long time, without even realizing why I was so exhausted to begin with.

We all know giving can be a beautiful habit.

However, if you do not include yourself in the giving process, it is incomplete.

I was always a giver. Giving comes easily to me. I know how to give and give and give some more. Often, I give until there is nothing left.

I felt like a cow being milked from too many sides, and after a while, there was no more milk to take.

I saw myself as lying flat on my belly—like a cow—my legs spread out, exhausted beyond belief. I didn't even feel like I had the energy even to get up. Still, I felt more people needed milk from me. I felt them reaching out to my teats, trying to get the last drop of energy out of me, and then walking away from me, disappointed that I was spent.

This was how I felt, until I learned to fill up my cup, too. Now I leave a little milk for myself.

I learned that I shouldn't only fill my cup after everyone else has had theirs and only if there is anything left—but to fill my cup first!

I learned to fill my cup first and let it overflow—and only after I felt filled up, I then shared with all my heart.

There is nothing better than sharing from a full cup, as you actually have the energy to truly enjoy giving.

We should earn to keep our cups filled up before we give to others. Always pour from a full jar.

I learned from my experience that I can never pour from an empty jar, no matter how much I want to. It seems so obvious, but it can be so difficult to learn, especially when you are used to being the one to give and take care of others. You have to learn to take care of yourself first.

I always was a giver. I always thought I had to give to earn love and approval, so giving comes easily to me still.

Even now that I feel like I've learned my lesson about filling my cup before taking care of others, I have to admit I still often fall back into the giving trap. It's just what I am used to. It's my lesson to learn, my *relationship pattern*.

However, since I started paying more attention to how my giving affected me, I catch myself earlier. I actually see when I am giving too much. I recognize my exhaustion earlier.

Learning to acknowledge when we are repeating old patterns is the key. We need to learn to check in with ourselves and to be aware of how we are thinking, feeling, and what we are doing. We have to ask ourselves how what we are doing feels to us: does it feel good to give, or are we getting tired and a little resentful, which is a clear sign we are over giving.

Learning to receive is another big step. I was so good at giving, but I never allowed myself to accept anything in return. Looking back, I see I did not really feel worthy of receiving, and often felt I needed to do something to even out the exchange, or I would feel indebted to the person who gave to me.

There was a period in time when I learned to receive. I was recovering from a severe ice skating accident. I was down with a concussion and whiplash, and could barely move. My kids were still young at the time, and I had to rely on help from others. Wow! Letting others help me was so uncomfortable at first.

The first time a friend brought around some cooked food, I nearly cried because I was so relieved and happy to get some help. Then I saw the smile on my friend's face and realized I was giving her a gift by receiving her amazing food. It actually felt good for her to give something to me.

And, surprisingly, accepting help—receiving—felt good to me. I was in a state where I couldn't do anything more than simply receive, to allow others to take care of me and to give to me.

It was a big a-ha moment for me, one caused by me being flat on my back. I hope you don't have to let it come this far to learn to receive help and support from others. You can allow others to feel joy when they give to you by being open to receiving.

If everyone always only gives, and there is no one open to receiving, whom would we give to?

So next time a friend offers to treat you to a coffee, smile and say, Yes! Thank you.

My kids still laugh at my 'discussions' about who would pay the bill when a friend wanted to invite me for lunch, and I didn't want to receive. In hindsight, it is hilarious, but perhaps I wasn't being very gracious.

So do a good deed by allowing someone to give to you. Be grateful for receiving. Remember that when you allow others to give to you, you receive a little bit of love from them.

When was the last time you allowed someone to treat you to a coffee, lunch, or theater tickets?

Wisdom From The Heart

Compliments are another way of receiving.

While we lived abroad, I realized that many people simply say thank you to a compliment, which felt odd at first. However, when I thought about it, their thank yous were far better than saying, "Yeah but..."

So this *Wisdom From Within* is a practice of accepting compliments, and learning to receive kind words from others fully, without negating them in any way.

Next time someone pays you a compliment, remember to

Smile

And simply say, "Thank you."

It might not feel right the first time around, and maybe not the second time around either. Just keep trying and remember to say *thank you* instead of *but* to a compliment.

Eventually, it will just become a habit.

This is a wonderful and simple way to practice receiving.

Have fun with it. There is no need to be harsh on yourself if you forget. We all stumble when we are learning. Be compassionate and loving towards yourself, like you would be with a toddler learning to walk or someone who you were teaching a valuable but hard to learn lesson.

I LOVE YOU

Is it important to say, "I love you"?

Oh yes, it is important to me to say, "I love you." I do it often with my kids. We have a little game: When I say or write "I love you," they say, "I love you more," and then I say, "You can't love me more because I love you so much more..." and on we go.

Every time my daughter and I connect on a call or on a chat, we share our love. Now that she is away at university, we feel more of an urge to say "I love you" when we are talking.

Saying "I love you" when we are sincere about it is amazing and feels so good. There are times, however, when we might say it just to hear it back, and then it has needy strings attached. Oh, I've done that too. Our urge to feel loved and hear that we are loved in return is powerful for many of us, and probably a survival mechanism.

When James and I were newly together, he told me "I love you" so often. I remember him standing at the bathroom mirror and turning to me, saying, "I love you. I won't let anything get in between us."

I was so happy at the time, but eventually, his ex-wife and many other things did get in between us, and that is OK too. Our relationship just wasn't meant to be.

I remember he told me "I love you" every single day, and so often that it was almost too much—it was laid on thick, so to speak.

Even though the words are wonderful and loving, it can feel like there are strings attached by the statement, or like a person actually means, "You belong to me," or "You make me happy."

When James said it to me so much, it just felt a bit off, but I still drank in the words and wanted them to be true.

I learned from previous experiences to only say "I love you'" or reply, "I love you, too," when I honestly felt called to do so. That meant I didn't always say, "I love you, too." Now I realize it was probably what James wanted to hear and the reason he told me that he loved me so often.

Saying "I love you" seems like it was part of James' sales game. Like I mentioned before, looking back, I see he was a salesperson and was very good at selling himself to me.

Trust within, how does it feel when someone says "I love you"? Does it feel sincere? If so, then take it in wholeheartedly. If not, let it go. Sometimes people try to manipulate us or to soften us with "I love yous."

Oh, kids are the best at this. When I said no to something my youngest asked me for, he asked,

"Don't you love me?" People might also try to guilt you into doing something for them, saying, "If you really loved me, you would…"

There are other signs of love that a person can give. A simple smile or a hug shows love, too.

James told me "I love you" often at the beginning of our relationship, but he said it less and less as the relationship progressed, and then I was the one saying it more and more towards the end of our relationship when the ship started sinking.

I remember how often I told him I loved him, and yes, I often said it just to hear from him that he still loved me too.

Just to feel reassured, that he wanted to stay with me.

Just to feel loved, even though his actions felt unloving.

Just to try to get back into that loving feeling with him.

Just to sustain the relationship, which was great at the beginning but saw too many hurdles and troubles to continue.

When I was happy and felt good about myself at the beginning of my relationship with James, I was more playful and loving towards myself as well. Towards the end of our relationship, I was so needy of love. I'd left parts of myself behind again, and feared feeling like a failure, having another relationship that I couldn't hold together. "What is wrong with me?" I wondered. "Why does no one love me? Why are they all leaving me?"

I hoped by saying "I love you" over and over again, I could work some sort of magic, and create a loving relationship again.

However, my declarations of love came from the wrong place—from a place of neediness, a place of not feeling good about myself, a place of lack. I did not feel loving towards myself, so I needed outside confirmation that I was worthy of love. If he would only tell me that he loved me, then I would know that I was lovable, I thought.

And truth be told, I did not truly love him. I loved the idea of love, the idea of being in a relationship.

All love is a journey—a journey within, a journey back to ourselves. It's a deep journey learning about what love is and what it means and how we actually love someone, or ourselves. We can walk this path too and remember we are love.

So you see, saying "I love you" is important when you truly feel it in your heart, not simply because you want to hear it back.

Also only say "I love you, too" when you truly feel it. Be honest with yourself, and also learn to just receive the words from someone else without feeling like you need to say it back. Let someone tell you from his heart, "I love you," and just breathe it in, let it stand, and receive it into your heart.

Nothing else is needed. "I love you" is a gift from one heart to another. No reply is truly necessary.

When did you last say I love you to yourself?

Wisdom From Within

If you have a hard time telling yourself "I love you," you are not alone.

Many people have a very hard time expressing their own love to themselves.

Just keep saying it to yourself; it gets easier every time, and you will learn that the greatest gift you can give yourself is to voice your love for yourself.

Stand in front of a mirror.

Look yourself into your eyes (keep doing for a couple of breaths, and expand it to minutes over time).

Connect to your soul by looking yourself into your eyes.

Connect to your heart.

And say out loud, "I love you."

Even better use your name: "I love you, (your name)."

Feel into this.

Keep looking into your eyes, connecting with your soul.

And say out loud again, "I love you (your name)."

Do this as many times as you need. I would say about seven times would be a fabulous start.

And then, of course, repeat this practice several times each

and every day.

Every time you pass a mirror, tell yourself, "I love you."

Enjoy sharing your love with yourself.
You are so worthy.

♥

CHRISTMAS

Is Christmas truly a celebration and season of love?

Yes, to me Christmas is a celebration of love and giving. It's the coming together of loved ones in its essence. Of course, modern consumerism has changed it a little, as has added the stress of getting everyone together in one place at one time. These things can take the focus off of the message of love that is at the center of Christmas.

Like with so many things in life, it is more about how you choose to celebrate that makes it loving. The little things you do can help you feel the love in Christmas again.

I always loved Christmas. I adore the tree, the presents (of course), and cherish the time of just being and relaxing with my family.

I have fond memories from my childhood: sitting around the tree, lighting candles (yes, we had real candles), listening to Christmas music, and receiving a doctor's case as a young child, which was my most treasured gift ever.

I remember playing games with my sisters, enjoying the new toys we got, and playing together until late in the evening.

I remember fondly sitting with my father and trying to guess which candle would go out last. I can still picture the shadow of the tree growing on the wall as the candles got smaller and smaller and eventually went out.

Christmas always held that place of love for me. It was a time when I could just be and enjoy the spirit of the season.

When my kids were younger, I loved to decorate the tree with them. Yes, sometimes it was a bit hectic, taking care of children and preparing for Christmas. I loved to bake cookies and decorate the house.

And I always loathed putting it all back away after Christmas, usually on January 6th.

Toni expected a perfect tree, a perfect dinner, and perfect presents. I usually got nice jewelry, though I actually treasured the self-made gifts from my children more than the expensive presents from my ex-husband.

Over time, the kids grew taller and older. Christmas presents were less about surprise, and school took up a lot of time for them.

Creating the perfect Christmas for everyone became exhausting for me, and I ended up feeling drained afterward. I realized I did not even feel like putting up a lot of decorations anymore; I was already thinking about having to take them back down again. Christmas became more of an inner journey for me.

I love to walk around Christmas markets near us. They just have a special energy.

I love sharing thoughtful gifts or writing cards

When the children were young, I used to send out perfect Christmas cards to 100s of people. Friends told me that ours was always the first card they got. They were always on time and included both a handwritten note and gorgeous photos of the children. Yes, you guessed it—this was during my marriage to Toni.

I refused to write to his work colleagues eventually, though. I just had so many cards to write and did not even know those people, so I asked him to write the cards for his colleagues himself. The request didn't sit well with Toni, though.

Christmas is not about sharing your perfections. To me, it is more about just being and connecting with the love within ourselves and the love around us. This is something to do in stillness, with inner peace and an open heart. We can never really connect to the love around and within us when we are too busy focusing on making everything perfect.

Christmas is special. Peaceful energy is heightened, and love is in the air. I learned to connect with that love more and more, by doing less and less.

We started having live Christmas trees that we could later plant in the garden.

Nowadays, we have a live tree we keep on the patio in a pot. We bring it in on the 24th, and my daughter, Catherine usually decorates it. On the 26th it goes out on the patio again, after we've taken the decorations off.

I don't decorate the house much anymore. Yes, I have candles that remind me of Christmas, and I love using throughout the year.

I have some special little trinkets I put out, and they are beautiful and enough.

Simplicity is key. Christmas is in our hearts, after all.

When my kids were young, I loved to celebrate *en famille* on the 24th, with just the kids and us parents. After Toni left, I still loved to celebrate just with my kids for one evening, as this time truly represents the Christmas feeling of home and love to me, and I treasure the time I spend with my kids.

During my marriage, we opened the circle to grandparents and aunts and usually had them at our house on the 26th.

Now that it is just my side of the family and the kids don't see their father or his side any longer (you can read more Christmas stories in my first book *Conversations With Me*), we play it by ear. One year we might celebrate at my mother's, another year she might be here with us.

I learned to keep it simple, do what feels right, and abandon all sense of what has to be done, what is proper, and how it is supposed to be celebrated.

Spending time with my children is my favorite way to celebrate this special season.

I remember one year of celebrating with my kids. We were cooking together in the kitchen after we opened our presents. I remember the sparkles in the eyes of my children, the flour on their faces, when we baked cookies, the hugs we shared. That is Christmas to me.

Feeling that love—the love we have for each other—cherishing that love and just being together is what is important to me. It's time to be home, time to breathe, and yes, spending time with my family that feels good. I don't need anything fancy. The simple things are more important to me.

Simplicity is love. When you know you are truly expressing love to the people around you, you don't need to show it off.

Christmas became more profound when I started to celebrate it the way I loved to, when I allowed it to be simple, when I allowed myself to choose and do it my way.

Years ago on a retreat, I did an exercise that led me to dive into my purpose. I felt I would love to be Santa, riding around the world and sharing chocolates. Then I realized chocolates symbolize love to me, and that I would be happy to share love with the world. Yes, Santa brings love to each and every one of us, if we let him.

I adore watching Santa movies; they always bring me back to love and show what love is all about and what Christmas is all about. Yes, Christmas is also about family movie time. That's another way we can be together, enjoying each other's company.

And, to me, the best time of the year is the time between Christmas and New Years. I love that time when the children are on holiday. I treasure the days when I can simply be, read a book, get up late, watch movies, and feel into each day as I go. It's a time of peace and quiet, and it feels as if time stands still.

When was the last time you enjoyed a simple Christmas holiday and feeling?

Wisdom From The Heart

You can find out what Christmas (or any other love holiday you celebrate) is all about for you.

Get some paper, pencils, crayons, art supplies, magazines, etc.

Ponder the question:
How does your favorite Christmas look?

Take a minute to breathe.

Close your eyes.

And let yourself dream.

How would YOUR perfect Christmas be?

How would it feel like?

What would you do?

Where would you be?

How does it look?

Who would be there with you?

How would it smell like?

What food would be there?

Who is cooking?

Are you ordering in?

What would you drink?

Would you listen to music? What kind?

Feel into each question and ask yourself any other questions that come up for you, too.

Dream your perfect Christmas.

When you are ready,

Open your eyes and create your perfect Christmas on paper:

Write it out.

Paint or draw it.

Or make a collage with cutouts from your magazines. Browsing through magazine and intuitively picking the pictures and words you like is also helping you tapping into your feeling of a loving Christmas.

Feel into it, and let this perfect Christmas grow within you.

You are allowed to celebrate your own way and make your own kind of Christmas.

It is *your* Christmas, *your* feeling of love.

Bring the love back to Christmas for yourself.

Remember you can be flexible and celebrate each year differently. See what works best for you and what feels right to you, and go with that.

GROW WITHOUT LOVE

Is it possible for people to grow without love?

No, absolutely not.

We are love; love is our true essence.

We came from love, and we are going back to love when we leave this life. While we play here on earth in our earthly bodies, we often crave the love from back home, that love we came from.

We crave it from our parents, and yes, most of them tried to do the best they could—remember they were also looking for that love themselves and might not have been aware of how to truly, unconditionally love, so many of us did grow up experiencing conditional love.

Parents might say things like, "When you behave like this, I can't love you," or, "Be a good girl." These statements make us feel like we need to work for love.

We came here to experience a learning process, learning how to give, receive, and be love. Remember, we all chose our paths, our parents, and our life circumstances before we came to earth. Yeah I know, it sometimes sucks, right? You might ask yourself, "Did I really choose this? How could I ever think this would be great to experience?"

So, while we all come from that big unconditional love where we are a part of that love, we come onto this earth with all its duality. We might end up missing that unconditional love we were a part of before—some of us more, some of us less. I am definitely one of the people who miss that love more.

In truth, we are love and we need love. Love is the core of who we are, though we have been waylaid and forgotten about it.

Back to your question: Can we grow without love?

Let me share a story with you, one I always found horrific. I heard it from our priest while I was attending confirmation lessons as a teenager. He shared the story of the tests that were done in a far away land in an orphanage years ago (probably 19th century even).

There was this orphanage with loads of babies. The nurses and caretakers were only allowed to do the necessities for the babies: feeding them, changing their diapers and clothes, and keeping the babies comfortable.

But they had to use facemasks and were not allowed to interact with the babies in any form.

No smiles, no words—nothing. They simply gave the infants basic food and care.

You know what happened to the babies?

They ALL died!

Yes, they did, and you know why? They died because they did not receive LOVE. Humans simply CANNOT grow in such a loveless surrounding.

What a terribly sad story, right? Who could do such experiments on human beings, or any living creature, to say the least?

So you see, we can't even *live* without love, let alone grow without it.

If we lack basic forms of loving interactions, like smiles, hugging, or positive attention, we die.

There were many similar experiments done on plants as well. If we talk with our plants, when we share love with them, they grow better. Even playing Mozart helps plants.

So if we can't grow without love, why do so many of us withhold love from ourselves? It's likely because we don't know better, because we don't even realize we are doing it.

So share the love with yourself. Let the love shine out of your heart. Share your love with the world.

Share it now. The world needs your love, and you need your love, too.

And just between us moms, yes, I can admit there were times when I withheld my love from my children (unintentionally) and now that I think about the story above now, I can see that I may have halted their growth for a little while.

Love doesn't mean we have to accept all behaviors and everything our children do; it simply means that withholding love is not a good form of punishment at all.

Love starts within each of us with the recognition and memory of our true essence. We are love, and love is all we are.

Everything else just falls away.

We might have put on a tough armor to shield us from the world or put many patches on our souls, we may have learned tactics to shield ourselves or keep us from getting hurt or giving too much... but deep down, we all come back to love.

We find our flow of love, our truth.

So the question, "How can we come back to love?" might be the big question here.

When was the last time you honestly felt love?

Wisdom From The Heart

How can you feel the love? There are a couple of things we can all do:

Use Rose

Roses carry the essence of love. So you can buy yourself some roses, take time to smell the roses on your way, get a rose quartz to carry around in your pocket (this stone is an amazing Heart Healer). Buy rose essential oils or perfume with a hint of rose. Pictures of roses are healing too.

I prefer pink roses, myself, as their energy is so gentle and loving.

Create Heart Space

Get back in your heart space by simply putting your hands on your heart and taking gentle breaths.

Breathe in love, be love, reconnect with love.

Connect to loving Mother Earth Energy

Ground yourself.

Put your bare feet on the grass or imagine you are standing on grass or moss.

Imagine roots growing down out of your feet

Breathe in the deeply nurturing, loving energy from the heart of the earth.

Fill your body with loving Mother Earth Energy from your feet all the way up to the crown of your head.

Breathe it in, filling your body with this energy.

And release anything that no longer serves you into the earth for transformation.

Remember you are supported, you are grounded, and you are loved.

Connect with Universal Love

Connect to the Universe through the crown of your head.

Imagine gorgeous white light filling your body

From head to toe.

Feel the love, and release anything that is not aligned with love.

Breathe and just be.

Feel the connection, the support, and the love from the Universe.

You are not alone and you are so loved.

TUSCANY

Is it possible to do too much for love?

Oh, absolutely! I know I often did too much for the sake of love. Giving myself up while trying to make Toni happy was just a part of it. There were other things I still feel I should have listened to my inner voice —my wisdom— about, as some things come back and hit you with a vengeance.

Of course, if what you do is for love and it feels right at the time, there is never too much you can do. Love just is. There is no quantity or quality to it.

We can all overindulge, though, and over-give in the hope of being loved in return.

One story I remember which is still laced with sadness and a sense of how silly I could be is the story of my dream of Tuscany.

Tuscany has been calling to me—I still haven't been there yet. I love all things Italian: I find Italian men very alluring; I love the language, which is so full of love; and the food—oh, the food is divine; and the way of life in Italy stirs my soul. Everything about Italy is somehow magical to me. I feel Italy is the country of love.

Have you ever been to Italy? If not, I highly recommend it! Go and do as the Italians do.

Back to Tuscany … it must be gorgeous there! The thought of the landscape and the cities is so appealing to me, and yes, there is amazing wine there, too!

Years ago, Toni and I had the opportunity to travel to Tuscany with a dear friend who knew his way around and was familiar with the best vineyards; however, it just didn't feel right for me at the time. Our friend was freshly in love. We would have been travelling to the country of love with smitten lovers, and I feared I would see the lack in my relationship with Toni even more clearly if we accompanied a happy couple, with the spirit of Italy all around me.

So I canceled that trip, and soon after Horatio broke his leg. He was only three years old at the time, so it was good that we weren't abroad. I feel it was another sign I was meant to stay home.

I'm still sad that I was not feeling it back then. It would have been amazing to see and experience Tuscany, especially with someone who knew his way around and had insider knowledge.

When I met James, he also wanted to go to Tuscany. Yes, I could see myself going to Tuscany with James, feeling the passion of the area, exploring our passion together, and feeling the love. We had a shared goal, or so it seemed.

When James moved in with me, he needed a lease contract. Of course, he was living in my home rent-free—the house was big enough, and everything was already set up. However, for his divorce proceedings, he needed proof that he was paying rent. Yeah, I think you see where this is going. So he set up a contract, and I—with love-struck trust—signed it. He had proof that he was paying rent, and we agreed that he would put the money aside that he should have been paying and use it to travel to Tuscany together. This felt good to me; it felt like we do this together.

However, we never made it to Tuscany. I am still disappointed. It would have been a dream come true.

Not only did we never make it to Tuscany, James never shared the money he was supposed to put aside for his 'rent'—not even when I was in desperate financial situations. For some reason, I could not make it clear to him that he would have to pay his share if he lived with a colleague or roommate.

The money wasn't the only issue that came up. As he had needed the contract for his divorce proceedings, his ex contacted my ex-husband, to verify our agreement and I was in deep trouble because Toni used this contract against me. Also, funnily enough, James blamed Toni instead of his ex or himself for the problems this caused.

Yeah, silly me. I never intended to hurt anyone. I just wanted to go and visit Tuscany. However, by signing the lease contract, I unleashed a boomerang that came straight back at me.

I only wanted to support James, and I never felt I was taking anything away from Toni. Still yes, by trying to help James, I did too much in the name of love.

I remember that it felt weird to me when I signed the contract. James pressured me and talked me into it. Later, when I said I wanted to see the contract again, he never showed it to me. It felt really off, but still, I did it just so he would stay with me—so I could have a man in the house. I felt that someone in love would support her partner in this way.

Of course, I learned from this experience. I know now that if I ever live together with a romantic partner again, we will be equal partners and we will share the rent.

It was a steep learning curve, and I think I needed this lesson only once.

Tuscany is still calling, and maybe one of these days I will go and visit it myself. I still long to feel the love of Italy, feel the love of love, and immerse myself in love.

Was there ever a time when you gave too much in the name of love?

Wisdom From The Heart

Forgiveness is important. Forgive yourself for all the things you have done wrong in the past.

You did those things meaning well, no matter what came out of them.

Now you know better, but back then, you did the best you could.

One of my favorites forgiveness practices is Ho'oponopono

Stand in front of a mirror.

Look yourself in your eyes.

Repeat these four sentences:

- I apologize.
- Please forgive me.
- I love you (your name).
- Thank you.

When you first start this practice, say the sequence seven times—it's a beautiful angel number—and say it to yourself whenever you see a mirror, or at least once a day.

You will feel better soon after you start this gorgeous forgiveness routine.

Be gentle towards yourself. You are only human, after all.

FAVORITE AUNT

How important is it to have loving parents?

This question is quite tricky for me to answer. I would say very; it is so essential that we feel the love from our parents, and that our first interaction on this planet comes from love—a gentle loving and caring relationship.

Then again, I know we all choose our parents and the experiences that come with them before we were born, so any parent we get is the perfect parent for us.

And I also know from my own experience as a mom that, as parents, we try our best. Sometimes we just don't do so well with the loving part because we are humans, too. We might unintentionally repeat the mistakes of our parents when we deal with our kids.

I sometimes realized that I heard my mom speaking out of my mouth when I was mothering, and I had to pause and realign my words with my own beliefs. Sometimes I used the same mothering techniques my mom used— the ones I promised myself I would never ever use even before I had kids. And sometimes, because I grew up in a setting that was based on conditional love, I didn't know any different and could only share conditional love with my children, too.

So the answer to the question, "How important is it to have loving parents?" is: Yes. In a way, it is important. On the other hand, though, looking back I see that it is also important to be compassionate towards our own parents and especially loving and compassionate towards our own kind of parenting.

I think it is more important that we experience love, and have at least one loving relationship with an adult role model as we grow up. It could be an aunt or uncle, grandparent, a neighbor, or the mother of a friend—anyone we feel truly connected with. We all have that one person we feel close to.

I remember I often felt unloved by my parents, or only loved when I was a good girl, when I did well, when my parent were proud of me, when they could show me off. It only felt like love was based on if I was intelligent, or good looking, or something else beyond my control.

Even as a young adult, I did not remember being loved for who I was as a child. One of my healer friends asked me to go back to a time when I felt loved, and I saw myself with my aunt and uncle—an aunt and uncle who were fun and totally accepting of me. They were the people who I felt loved me no matter what. They loved me for who I was, not only when I did well or when I was a good girl.

So you see, I had love when I was growing up. I had people I could just be myself around. I also know that they could enjoy the time we spent together. I wasn't with them all of the time, and my mom had other children to watch over aside from me.

My mom loves me; I know that now. She was (and still is) very harsh toward herself, so it has always been more complicated for her to show me love, as it felt more like tough love. I am truly grateful for the experience of her love now. If it weren't for the way she showed me love, I would not have gone on this beautiful and most amazing journey to reconnecting with the love within myself, the loving journey of a lifetime. I would not have been able to learn what I have about love and about myself, or to experience it all and arrive at being me, the loving Caroline I am today. Yes, I did choose my mom perfectly, and I hope she, too, can find compassion and love for herself one day.

While going through my journey and the times I felt deeply unloved, I sometimes resented my parents for not loving me the way I needed to be loved. I knew deep down, it always takes two—that love is a relationship—but I wasn't satisfied with the love my parents were able to give me. I wanted more. I so needed to be loved—to feel loved—even as a little girl.

So while I was going through my heartaches and breakups, I still had that light, the light of the love I felt whenever I was with my wonderful aunt. It was the same love I felt as a girl, as a teen, and then, much later, as a grown woman. It was acceptance that felt like I was enough, that I was perfect just the way I was. Yes, I have this very special relationship with both my aunt and my uncle. They are both inspirations to me, and I am truly blessed to have them in my life as guiding lights showing me the way towards love.

Thank you, Aunt and Uncle. I love you very much.

And yes, Mom, I love you very much too. You are my mom and that will never change. Love is never comparing; it's not that I love your sister more. It's just that I resonated with her love more—it was more on my wavelength. I know you love me, too.

And sometimes we just have a special affection towards some people. I had it with other children too; some I could just relate to more, and some felt harder to connect with.

Embracing the love from your parents is part of a forgiveness process, part of a journey toward acceptance, and part how we learn about compassion.

Have you started to reconcile with the love from your parents? I highly recommend it, as they were the first people in your life when you arrived on earth. If you can't find a deep understanding within yourself for their situations and where they came from, you might not ever be able to heal fully and connect to the love within yourself. Even more important, you might never fully grow into being the best parent you want to be for your own children, and in turn, helping your children to grow into the best parents they can be for your grandchildren.

We can never truly be free as long as we carry a grudge, resentment, or pain from our childhoods into our adult lives.

Now is the time for you to set yourself free. Do it not only for yourself, but also for your children and all the future generations to come.

Remember you are so worth it.

Are you ready to heal from your past?

Wisdom From The Heart

Forgiveness and acceptance are great ways to start healing.

I am deeply fond of the Serenity Prayer, and I found this alternative based on the original:

My favorite Serenity Prayer:

God, grant me the serenity to stop beating myself up for not doing things perfectly,

The courage to forgive myself because I'm working on doing better,

And the wisdom to know that you already love me just the way I am

Unknown

I truly love this kind of *Serenity Prayer*. If it resonates with you, you can use it as often as you feel is needed.

♥

NITS AND LICE

Are self-love and self-worth connected?

Oh yes, they are very much connected. You see, when you don't feel worthy, you can't love yourself, and as long as you don't love yourself, you can't feel worthy either. Self-love and self-worth go hand-in-hand. The more you love yourself, the more worthy you feel.

I never felt worthy of love, and let my partners manipulate me—and unfortunately, my kids, too.

One day, James came home and told me he had gotten a call from his ex-wife informing him that his son had lice.

"Oh no," I thought. I ran to check all three of my kids, as I feared they could have gotten lice from his son.

My kids' heads were free of lice and nits, so I took a deep breath and relaxed.

Then James said that his son must have gotten lice from my kids.

I looked at him and told him that my three had no lice, so it was impossible for his son to have gotten it from us.

James was adamant. You see, his ex-wife told him that their son had gotten lice from my children, and she was angry about it.

I remember James standing in the kitchen, telling me there must be some way for my kids to have given his son lice.

I stood there, my mouth open—flabbergasted—looking at him, and thinking, "I am in the wrong movie here." I told him, "It is impossible for my three to have given your son lice because they don't have any lice and nits, themselves."

He still felt there must have been some way for it to happen. He only saw what he wanted to see, and tried to find a way to make it plausible.

He would not let my argument stand, and no logic could get into his head.

I was getting angry and I went to my bedroom.

I was angry that I let him and his son into my life so easily, while his ex-wife was taking every opportunity to blame my kids and me for anything and everything.

I was angry that my kids were nearly infected with lice from his son.

I was angry that James could not accept the simple facts.

I was angry that I could not make him see reason.

I was angry that James never took our side of an argument. He always sided with his ex-wife and blamed us.

Yes, I was angry. Unfortunately, my need to be in a relationship won out over my need to be right, and I gave in to him and his reasoning.

I know now that my anger was a sign that something was not right in our relationship. I felt unheard, unseen, and left alone.

Our relationship had started that way, too. Somehow his ex got my phone number and started sending me really nasty text messages.

I never responded, but I feared the next attack from her. Back then, I had no idea how to step up and stop her messages or block her, and I also felt it was *his* place to tell her to stop. I knew she was just like a spoiled child, discarding her husband, but not letting any other girl play with him.

Being under constant verbal and emotional attack while James lacked the nerve to confront his ex didn't help our new love.

I could feel the resentment building; I could feel her lashing out at me with every fiber of my body. I never met her in person, but her messages to me were enough to stop me from desiring to meet her.

I understood, in a way, that James wanted to protect his son; however, I see things from a different perspective now and know that James' lack of clarity and sympathy toward his ex-wife wasn't really helping his son, either. He just enabled his ex to use their son as a tool against him and as bait for arguments between us.

If you are in a relationship where you or your partner still have unfinished business with an ex-spouse, take a time out to clarify boundaries, rectify issues, and think about how you need to move forward. Otherwise, it's not fair to anyone involved.

I know hope springs eternal, and I tried to remain confident that things would get better. It might have for others, but it never did for us.

Be careful, especially if you get blamed for unreasonable things or sense that your partner's ex is being manipulative. Set up clear boundaries for yourself, discuss some boundaries with your partner, and see whether your partner can hold to the boundaries with his ex—or get the hell out of there.

Unhealthy relationships have a way of playing tricks on us. Like when I tried to use common sense and explain to James that there was no way his son could have contracted lice from mine if mine were louse-free. I could not get through to him; he was so in line what his ex told him—his son had gotten lice from us—that there *must* have been a way for that to be true in his mind. He wasn't interested in logic.

All was lost, and stayed lost. It's good for me this relationship with James dissolved eventually. There is only so much a person can bear.

I also remember the time when I asked myself, "Am I mad, or is he?" That is a clear sign of an unhealthy relationship.

This incident was towards the very end of our relationship; it was about the Pentecost weekend. James promised to spend the weekend with us and then, a week later, he told me he was seeing his son.

I asked, "Do you remember you said you would come here?" He was so mad. He screamed at me, and yes, he bullied me. He told me he had never said anything like that, and he was always planning to see his son and on and on.

I just shut up. As a sensitive soul, as an Empath, I can't deal with people shouting at me, especially when they are being so mean and trying to blame me.

I remember standing there, and wondering if I was making things up or if he was conveniently forgetting plans we'd made.

I know his ex-wife probably changed plans again and wanted him to have his son. Still, that was no reason to scream at me and make me feel like I was at fault. It is possible for people to change plans and stay reasonable and talk about it.

Love, self-love, and self-worth are all interconnected.

As long as we don't truly love ourselves, feeling that deep love for ourselves and feeling worthy of love, we take on shit from partners. We don't feel worthy of being loved, and we choose partners who mirror this belief. They will show us we are not worthy, and not lovable; they bend us more and more, till we break free.

It is not unusual for Empaths, Sensitive Souls, Lightworkers, and Earth Angels to enter unhealthy relationships. We have a deep longing to help others. We see broken souls and, instead of being their coaches, we take them as our partners in romantic relationships and close friendships with the aim of helping and healing them. They don't want to be helped or healed, though; in their eyes, nothing is wrong with them. With a healthy dose of self-love and self-worth, we are less susceptible to get involved in or stay in such unhealthy relationships. We know that we deserve love and that we deserve much better friendships and relationships.

So save your need to help someone and start helping and healing yourself.

Learn to recover from unhealthy relationships, allow yourself to take the journey within, connect with yourself, and be more loving towards yourself.

You deserve your own love more than anyone else.

Is it time for you to start loving yourself, too?

Wisdom From The Heart

If you are unsure whether you are in a healthy relationship or not, take a step back, feel into your heart and look at it from an outside perspective.

Do you still have friends? (Isolation, estrangement from friends and family is a sign of an unhealthy relationship.)

Ask your close friends and family members:

Do you feel I have changed since I have been with this partner? (Find out whether you like to fit in and are bending over backwards or if you lost your shine.)

What do you think about my partner? (Be aware that partners who aren't kind to us can be the most charming people to others. So if your partner is outdoing himself to charm others and showing his mean side to you, it is still a sign of an unhealthy relationship.)

Be open to discussing your fears about your partner with your friends and family. Ultimately, though, you have to make the final call about staying in an unhealthy relationship.

Contact helplines and groups to get support for leaving your relationship, if that is what you want. You are not alone.

Sending you warm hugs. Even though you might not feel worthy, you deserve so much more! Ending an unhealthy relationship might hurt, but it shouldn't be the end of life.

♥

SELF-CARE OR SELF-LOVE

Aren't self-care and self-love the same?

Not really. You know, when you apply self-care, you are showing love for yourself; yes, that is true and vice versa, too. When you love yourself, you naturally integrate more self-care rituals into your life.

So, in a way they go hand-in-hand; however, they are not the same thing.

Self-care is something you do for yourself to nurture or take care of yourself. Baths, massages, time in peace and quiet, walks in nature, as well as healing methods like; Yoga, Qigong, meditation, Ho'oponopono, clearing your energy system, or going for a healing session are all self-care practices. There are so many more possibilities for self-care that really depend on a person's taste and abilities. Each of us knows best what is right for us and will choose self-care practices according to our needs. So I invite you to go deep within and find out what you need right now to feel better.

Self-care is more than just baths and massages, though. It expands in all areas of your life; it is part of leading a healthy lifestyle and looking after yourself, avoiding sickness and overwhelm.

Self-care is taking a break to just be and breathe. It's time to catch up with ourselves and our needs—and time to recharge, to go within, and be in the moment.

Remember: you can't pour from an empty jar.

Self-care helps you make sure that you are full of energy and able to take care of others and yourself.

Self-love, on the other hand, is a feeling you have, a deep acceptance and understanding for yourself, deep compassion for all aspects of your life.

Self-love is embracing all of yourself—not just the good parts—but everything: every cell in your body, every thought in your mind. It's about seeing yourself as a whole and loving yourself completely.

Self-love is being true to yourself, allowing yourself to be different and unique—to just be you. Understanding, compassion and love for all of who you are is what self-love is. It's not only accepting, but embracing who you are—no matter what—finding a way to integrate left and right, top and bottom, inside and out, the good and the bad. It's feeling compassion for the path you took, looking back over the way you came to where you are with pride and in awe.

It's sometimes like being an eternal mother, loving yourself just because you are you. Feeling that motherly understanding compassionate nurturing love for yourself is self-love. The feeling is something deep and nourishing.

So *self-care* is something we do and integrate (hopefully) in our daily lives. *Self-love* is a feeling, a deep sense of compassion and understanding for ourselves, no matter what.

Self-care can change from day-to-day, according to our needs. One day, we might need time alone in nature, while another time we feel called to have a cup of coffee with friends, then on another day, we might need a spa day or a day at the beach.

It is important to learn to apply our own kind of self-care, to listen within to find out what we need in the moment.

Self-care is more than having a cup of tea every day at 9 am. It is good to integrate good, healthy habits into our self-care routines; however, keeping a rigid structure can go against what self-care truly is.

Sometimes self-care is having a good cry. Yes, that is self-care, too. Crying allows the feelings to come up and be released.

Self-love just is.

So you see, *self-love* and *self-care* are indeed two different things. One might lead to the other, but they are different; one is a feeling and the other is habits or things we do to care for ourselves.

Which is more important, one might wonder. Neither. Both are equally important to lead a happy and joyful life.

As we can't have one without the other, just start someplace.

Apply a dose of self-love daily

And remember to take time for self-care on a daily basis, too.

When was the last time you had a Self Care day?

Wisdom From The Heart

Set yourself a reminder, maybe once every hour (you can do this easily nowadays on your smartphone)
When your timer goes off, or your alarm reminds you,
Sit quietly
And simply breathe.
Breathe into your belly.
Allow yourself to come back to yourself.
Breathe deep and exhale all the stress.
Breathe in more and exhale all the *must dos.*

Then concentrate on your heart.
Put your hands or fingers on your heart area.

Keep on breathing
And resting in your heart space.
Keep doing this simple exercise a couple of times a day

And you will realize that you get a better feeling of yourself.
You will get a better sense of what you need and how lovely you are.

When we are in our heart space
We feel the peace, the love and us.
Enjoy.
And let me know how you are doing.

ALLOWING YOURSELF TO RECEIVE

How easy was receiving for you?

Oh, receiving was a foreign concept to me for most of my life. I was a giver. Being generous and helping others was so easy and natural to me.

Receiving, however, didn't feel comfortable to me.

Looking back, it likely had to do with not feeling worthy, coupled with a need to always be the one who was being generous.

When a friend wanted to pay for my coffee, I would not let her; otherwise, I felt I would be in debt to her.

Remembering who paid what, and whom I needed to treat the next time was just too much to keep track of, and it took away from the happiness of receiving.

Also, I was always a self-made woman. I could take care of myself. I didn't need help or someone to pay for my coffee for me, right?

Oh, little did I know that receiving is the most amazing and healing gift you can get.

I fought receiving. I had lively discussions with friends about who was allowed to pay for dinner or an evening out, and yes, my kids still love talking about those conversations. Even at times when I didn't have much and had to pinch every penny, I could not allow someone else to pay for the pizza. Knowing how hard it can be to earn money, how could I let my friends waste their money on me? No, I'd rather pay it myself. Also, if I paid for myself, I could choose exactly what I wanted without having to worry that being treated would cost a friend too much.

Do you see where this is going? Yes, I had a deep feeling of unworthiness.

I don't know where my low self-worth feeling came from—it does not matter. We don't need to know why or how. We only need to release the feeling, heal ourselves and come back to our centers.

Yes, I remember often feeling low. Toni used to tell me how unworthy I was, and I took his words to heart. I was open to his message. Of course, it didn't help my confidence to hear how unworthy I was over and over again.

When I realized how unworthy of receiving I felt and how much I was giving, I saw I had to heal parts of myself.

Also, I needed a knock on my head—quite literally— to finally be able to open up to receiving, partially because I had no other choice.

It took me being laid flat with a concussion and whiplash, like I mentioned in a previous chapter, before I could finally allow myself to receive help and support.

I could not cook, I could not drive, I could not shop; I could barely do anything more than lie in bed.

That's when friends showed up, ringing our doorbell, bringing over dinner, cookies, and more. Their help was such a relief to me and I got to see how their giving me help was actually a gift to them as well.

I was even able to ask for a favor. When one of my friends asked me whether she could help, I asked her if she would be able to fetch my car, which was still parked outside the ice rink. And yes, she was happy to fetch my car together with her husband, and they brought it back to my house for me.

I was so deeply grateful, as I had no way to go and get it myself, and didn't want to let it stand there for weeks or months. Just the thought of going to pick it up was too much for me to deal with at the time, as I couldn't drive because of the concussion and whiplash.

I was down for the count, laid flat for a good long time.

When I opened the door and let my friend in who brought yummy lasagna for my family to eat, I cried. I was so happy to get her help—so relieved and deeply grateful. I saw in her eyes how much she loved giving to me, and at that moment, I realized that:

By receiving, I allowed someone else the gift of giving.

In a way, I was giving too.

I had to be down and at my wits' end to finally be able to allow myself to receive. I had blocked and restricted myself so much that I never allowed myself the graceful feeling of receiving.

It is all a flow—giving and receiving, breathing in and out, day and night, flood and ebb … I had to experience it my own way, though.

Yes, I would have preferred not to knock my head so hard, but I can assume the Universe sent me gentler signs before my accident, and I just did not listen.

Do you receive easily?

I, for one, know receiving is not easy for many— that is till they've allowed it, and then it comes more naturally. If we think about how good it feels to give and remember that we are, in fact, giving a gift to the other person. By learning to receive gracefully, we are giving our friends the gift of giving.

During the time I was laid up in bed, I was thinking, "What if we were all givers, and no one was allowed to receive? Whom would we give to?"

Learn to allow yourself to receive. The more you allow yourself to receive, the more you allow yourself to accept the gift of love, too.

You see, I was not only blocking myself from accepting gifts and help from others, but I was also blocking myself from receiving and feeling love from my friends and family.

When was the last time you were able to receive something and simply say, "Thank you"?

Wisdom From The Heart

Receiving is a heart opening experience.

You can practice it by doing the following:

Sit someplace quiet.

Breathe in.
Breathe out.
Now breathe into your heart.
And breathe out through your heart.
Breathe into your heart again.

Imagine your heart opening wider with each breath.

Keep breathing IN to your heart
Allowing all the good to flow to you.

Breathe in the love.
Breathe in the support.
Breathe in the gifts.
Breathe in the blessings.
Breathe in sunshine.
Breathe in all of the positive feelings and
experiences you need.

Keep breathing in to your heart

And you will be able to receive more and more.

Enjoy receiving. You are so worth it.

LIKE MOTHER, LIKE DAUGHTER

Does what we do influence our children?

Yes, of course. For a long time, I told my children what to do, that is until I learned they don't follow our words, they copy our behaviors.

Back when I was married, I was a pleaser, and I let everyone walk all over me.

My daughter was bullied at school and had a hard time with mean girls.

I could not say no; she could not say no.

I could not stand up for myself; she couldn't either.

Even though I told her to stand up for herself and not let people treat her badly, my words did not mean a thing, as I was not living them myself. I wasn't showing her how to stand up for herself.

I remember how I cried when she came home. She was such a sensitive and kind girl at the age of six or seven. She asked me for five Francs. I asked her why she needed it.

She then told me that a girl in class told her to bring five Francs to school the following day and then the girl would be her friend for a day.

I was stunned. I had no idea how mean little girls could be.

Why would my kind, friendly, loving daughter need to buy friends?

Couldn't she just leave those girls and find some who liked her for who she was?

Yeah, like I was hanging around people who liked me for whom I was.

I wanted my daughter to be stronger than I was, even though I was not showing her how to be strong and assertive.

I was not standing up to my husband. I was not saying no. I let myself be treated badly, and yes, I probably felt like I was paying dearly for the honor of being married. I felt like it was my job to try harder and give more to keep our marriage together.

I did not give her the five Francs, not then or any other time.

I felt sorry for her, and I knew we needed to take her out of that school—out of an unhealthy situation, where she would be stuck with the same mean, so-called friends for another four years.

I cried when the wonderful teacher at the new school came to me and asked me what had happened to my daughter.

I felt shocked to hear how she would cringe every time she had to participate in class or say something. The teacher told me that Catherine would look around left and right expecting a mean remark or a rebuff from a classmate.

Luckily, that teacher could sense my daughter was fearful and helped Catherine fit in and feel more comfortable. She knew that she could not call on Catherine to give an answer in class; she knew Catherine was still too fragile.

Over time, Catherine healed and grew stronger.

Halfway through that first year when Catherine was at her new school, Toni and I split up, and I was taken out of an unhealthy situation, too.

I could develop. I could heal. I could strengthen myself.

I realized, years later when I saw my daughter saying no so clearly to classmates, when she knew what she wanted, when she had clarity and strength and self-esteem—she needed to see me stand up for myself so she could learn to stand up for herself, too.

And then I looked at myself and realized how far I had come.

Yes, I learned to say *No;* so did she.

Yes, I learned to be myself; so did she.

The more I embraced myself for who I was, the more she could embrace herself, too.

So you see, by being more loving towards ourselves, we teach our children the most important lesson: to be love, and that we are all love and lovable.

We don't teach this lesson by using words, but by living it fully.

So our behavior is not only in our genes, but it is also a result of our upbringing, in the role models we see, and in what we are able to recognize and heal during our journey here on earth.

Nowadays, I am so very proud of Catherine. She is truly walking her path with courage and strength—and so am I, and my boys are, too.

Catherine has influenced me as well. When I saw how she could say no, I allowed myself to say no more often. Seeing her walking her path allowed me to walk my path more confidently.

So we actually influence each other in a way, as long as we as mothers are open to allowing our children to be our teachers.

How can you allow yourself to be influenced by your child(ren) today?

Wisdom From The Heart

We are all mirroring each other.

For a long time, I hoped to help my kids avoid feeling the pain I felt as a child, and to help them avoid making the same 'mistakes' I had made.

This was until I realized they don't see it the same way. They sometimes don't feel the same, even if they face a similar situation. They are here to make their own experiences.

How could I prevent my children from learning and growing? How could I hold them back from gaining life experience?

So allow yourself to see your children as their own human beings—not simply as your child(ren)—but also as your greatest teachers.

What is your child's most annoying habit?

What is irritating you?

What do you love most about your children?

What do you feel they are best at doing?

Consider the first two questions first. Yes, I know we might want to dwell on the good things about our children, but we learn so much more from the things that irritate or annoy us.

Sit with your answers, and feel into yourself.

Where—in you—do you have the same tendencies?

Where—in life—are you acting like them?

What are you trying to hide from them, from yourself, or from the world?

Allow the answers to come

And clear and heal those parts in you.

UNCONDITIONAL LOVE

Can we truly experience unconditional love?

You know, we live in duality on this earth. We came here to experience this duality, to feel our bodies and the restrictions of those bodies. We notice the difference between dark and light, feel the warmth and cold, experience the joy and pain, and deal with the ups and downs of life. We came to experience everything, including love and heartbreak.

Unconditional love is where we came from, and where we go back to when we transition from this life. Unconditional love is our souls floating in love. There are no restrictions— there is only love.

We came to this earth to grow, and we grow through our experiences here, which come primarily from feeling disconnected from unconditional love. We experience love as mostly conditional, and we—as much as we may hope to share unconditional love— usually end up sharing love with conditions attached. The situations we face come with our experiences here on earth—through our bodies, our beings, and our incarnations.

We weren't meant to come here to experience unconditional love, no matter how much we want it. Yes, I do know a thing or two about wanting to go home, back to that eternal, unconditional, glorious love. Many of us do.

We came here to experience this longing for unconditional love, and often we feel like we are doing something wrong because we can't love unconditionally. Please be aware, though that we are here to share our love as best as we can, and that is good enough. We aren't meant to share or receive unconditional love, as that is what we have in the afterlife.

We can come close to unconditional love in this lifetime, on this earth.

Are you a perfectionist too?

I think we all are perfectionists in one way or another and we can be very harsh on ourselves for not loving unconditionally, all of the time.

Rest assured though, the love you give is real—it exists, even if it isn't perfect. Love simply is. It is enough to love with a full and open heart, and it is only human to love some people less sometimes. We are all only human, after all.

The first time I heard the song, Human, by Christina Perry on the radio, I cried. It was such a relief to hear someone sing my feelings. Oh, I am human, OK. It felt like such validation to my being. I always strived to be superhuman by doing more than what I came here to do, more than I was even capable of doing as a human. "I am only human after all," was such a liberating thing to hear. Yes, I am allowed to make mistakes. Yes, I am allowed to feel human. She sings:

"I can do it,
but I am only human…
I can only take so much
Until I've had enough…"

So love and keep loving. Don't judge your love. Keep giving your love, keep healing and clearing your heart, and love more and more. The more you heal and the more you clear, the deeper you can love.

There were times when I felt I was pretty damn close to unconditional love, if only for a moment or a fraction of a second. It was worth it in its entirety.

When I held my babies just after they'd been born, they were so precious, and I felt so deeply loving, so thrilled, so amazed. Yes, I felt an outpouring of love to the tiny human beings I held in my arms—that grew in me. I felt that feeling of unconditional love every time I met each one of my three. Yes, holding a precious newborn is such a feeling of love.

Those newborns came from the love we all come from. They are darling and we feel the love coming from them. We might even feel overwhelmed by the love we feel for them, no matter whether it is a baby of our own, one we adopt, or a family member or friends' baby.

And even later on, when hugging my children, enjoying the moment, feeling the pride and love I had for them— yes, that's pretty close to unconditional love for me, always.

The love we feel for animals, and our pets are another gorgeous reminder of unconditional love. My dog, Goldie, greets me and wets the floor because she is always so excited when I come home.

Looking into her gorgeous eyes, feeling that love between us, is just amazing, and yes, I think it is pretty close to unconditional love. The moments she puts her head on my lap are priceless, sheer bliss.

When I see her run over fields, rolling in the snow, having so much fun, catching a ball, I connect to the playful, happy side within me.

Many days when I feel a bit down or tired in the morning, I feel refreshed and back in the flow after my walk with my dog. Just observing her amazing energy puts the joy back into my heart.

Our cat is also a fabulous example of pure love. When he comes and wants to be caressed, or when he just lies in the sun, he is teaching me so much about self-care and about looking after myself. Hearing the purring of our cat, feeling his soft fur, and seeing his bliss in just being himself makes me realize that unconditional love comes from him, too.

Our tortoises are less for cuddles, but more of a reminder of taking in the seasons, enjoying and growing with the bliss of the warming sunshine, allowing myself to hibernate and to go with the seasons. Also, observing those amazing animals, seeing them speeding around their cage or lying there soaking in the sun is also love.

So you see, we can come close to unconditional love; however, we should not punish ourselves if we can't hold the feeling for too long, or if the fact that we are human gets between us and the experience of unconditional love.

Do we judge a rainbow for having a variety of different colors? Do we ask the rainbow to only glow in one particular color?

Allow your love to flow and be a gorgeous rainbow in your days. Let your love shine in all the colors and add sparkle to the world around you. Your love is enough, now and forever.

Have you had moments of near unconditional love?

Wisdom From The Heart

Let's go back to one moment when you felt the unconditional love.

Maybe it is a memory of cuddling with grandparents, aunts, or your children or a pet.

Sit somewhere quietly.

Breathe in.

Allow yourself to relax.

Breathe out.

And allow your mind to wander to a time when you felt unconditional love.

Just let it come to you.

Allow this moment to share itself with you, a memory, a feeling, a knowing, a sense...

Feel into it.

Breathe it in.

Expand that feeling.

Breathe it into your whole body.

Breathe it into your heart and every cell of your body.

And anchor that love within.

Remember you can come back to this place anytime you wish.

Take another deep breath.

Give thanks to the moment and the people or animals involved.

And come back to the here and now.

We all carry those fabulous memories with us, and we can always tap into them, as we forget so often during our busy days, that we are all love.

♥

HUMAN BEINGS, NOT HUMAN DOINGS

That's a great saying, but what does it mean?

I know it is a gorgeous saying. Let me tell you, though, just *being* is pretty hard. We are all so conditioned for *doing* things. Yes, even as little children, we were praised for doing things like smiling, walking, and talking.

At school, we were told we needed to do our homework; we were praised for good work.

Did you ever hear, "Do your homework first, and then you can go out and play"? I heard that from my mom, and I heard it come out of my mouth when I was speaking to my children, too. Yes, we often repeat what our parents did, whether we want to or not. Realizing that we do repeat patterns is half the work.

So I grew up in the system that only allowed me to have some fun after my chores were done, as most of us did.

When I was just sitting and being (resting, allowing myself just to BE), then all those voices went off in my mind, saying things like:

- You are so lazy!
- Hey! Why are you just sitting around?

- Don't you have anything to do?
- The house doesn't clean itself!
- And other urges to do more.

Oh, this is nasty talk and it sure made me uncomfortable with myself for resting. Who wants to be called lazy?

So just *being* is no easy task.

I was taught this from childhood on. My mom was always busy, always doing something. Later, when I became a mom myself, I found there was always something to do, especially with younger children. Yes, it seemed that the minute I put my head on my pillow, one of them started crying again.

I was so in that *doing* mode. I had no way to stop, and really, when we sit in our living rooms and notice the dirt or mess around us, we feel like we'd better get up, right?

This can go further. A person might feel tired, exhausted, or even be sick, then hear her mother's voice: "A mom is never sick." Yeah right, a mother has no time to be sick.

Of course, we try our best to take care of our homes and to take care of ourselves when we are sick. We might try and get a little snooze in here and there, but this is not healthy. In the short-term, we might be able to manage, but over time, pushing ourselves through no matter how we feel will lead to exhaustion and burn out.

When my children were older and going to school, I still did not allow myself just to be. There was constantly something to do: laundry, cook, shopping, sorting through clothes and toys to get rid of the worn out, outdated, and outgrown items in our house.

We are also very good at distracting ourselves by keeping ourselves busy. We fear idleness, because it might lead to us discovering or thinking about some deep inner truth we might not want to deal with.

So if you realize you are keeping yourself busy all the time, take a break and dive deep. Ask yourself questions like, "Why is this showing up? What am I not willing to look at?"

Somehow, many generations ago we were infected with the 'doing disease.' Sitting still was deemed negative, unworthy, and lazy.

Who would want to lose precious time by merely sitting around?

So, just being is truly not an easy task. We've been socialized against allowing ourselves time to relax and just sit and rest.

When I was learning to be, I had so many excuses for not allowing myself just to do it—I mean to just be. Can we 'do' being?

Are we finally, as a society, learning how to sit down, rest, and allow ourselves to simply be?

Oh yes, so much stuff still comes up when we aren't being productive and spending every minute working or doing something. We feel like we are lazy and unworthy. We hear our inner voices screaming at us, and yes, we have plenty of excuses and reasons why we can't simply *be*.

That is the greatest part of it, though. If we listen to the voices, if we sit with them—without getting back into the doing mode—we learn so much about ourselves, and we can finally heal.

That recognition and wisdom allow us to work on healing the negative motivations and fears we have of how we will be seen by others—and by ourselves—if we allow ourselves to simply be.

We have to clear through eons of teachings and our upbringings, we have to release social and parental instructions, and we have to wade through murky waters to come to ourselves, or to find the place inside of each of us that is waiting for us when we can simply be.

Did you ever allow yourself just to be?

Most of us are the slaves to our own need to be doing something, the need to prove we are worthy by doing even better or more, or we stay busy to distract ourselves from what lies within.

Deep down, we have the fear that we are not lovable just for simply existing, for being who we are.

From the tender age of just a few weeks old, we learn our parents coo over us for smiling. When we started babbling, our parents clapped their hands. When we took our first steps, we felt the awe from our parents, and so on.

Could we ever just be? Were we ever praised for our ability to relax and take a break?

That's impossible, right? Only lazy people just sit around.

No wonder yoga, meditation, and all the other practices that help us to come back to ourselves are so popular, in a time when busyness has taken over.

We all strive for more, faster, and better. We feel like we have to do it all, ourselves.

At the same time, though, our souls, hearts, bodies, minds, and spirits are looking for less action, calmer days, and more time to explore within and gain a more profound knowledge of the world around us and ourselves.

Have you heard your soul calling for a bit of peace, a bit of simply being, too?

You are not alone. The trick is to go through all the uncomfortable feelings you have when you decide to make the change and allow yourself to 'practice' just being.

How do you do that? You can practice:

Allowing yourself to just be yourself, to be uniquely you.

Allowing yourself to feel worthy, just for being you,

Releasing and clearing everything that is coming up, while you are focused on being you.

Becoming more and more yourself by allowing yourself to merely be who you are in stillness.

Being has become a moment of truth.

By simply being, we clear all the chatter—the murkiness around our thoughts and our hearts—and we arrive at a clear mountain lake, calm, at peace, and deeply rested.

So yes, we are human beings; however, because of societal and family influence, and also internal drive and a desire to be worthy, we might have tried to be human machines, and more often than not, we overdid it.

Can you allow yourself to simply be?

Wisdom From The Heart

Sit somewhere comfortably
And simply be.
Notice what thoughts come up.
Notice what your eyes are doing.
Notice what you hear.
Notice what you feel.
Notice what you smell.
Notice what you taste.
Keep sitting and noticing.
How comfortable is it, simply being?
What is coming up?
Just notice it
And go back to being some more.
Allow things to come up, but only notice the thoughts and sensations, like an outside observer.
And keep doing this exercise. Make it a point to do it for longer stretches as you go along.
Strengthen your 'being muscle'.

I know we all try and escape being one way or another.
What is your way?

FATHERS

How important is a father in a girl's life?

Oh, a father's love is so very important in a girl's life. You see, I honestly believe that a father is a girl's first love. Women often marry men who are similar to their dads—at least I did.

Toni was intelligent (not in an emotional way) and listened to classical music, just like my father. He was 14 years older than me, like my father was 12 years older than my mom, though that's about all of the similarities between my father and my ex-husband.

My father was sensitive—highly so—and he was deeply compassionate and gentle. Toni seemingly had no emotional intelligence whatsoever.

Yes, it seems that I did not choose my husband too well. My marriage to Toni was an experience—a learning curve—it was a part of my path, and I wouldn't be the woman I am now without him.

So you see, in my eyes, my father was the perfect spouse to my mother. In my eyes, my father was the love of my life. Yes, I know he had his dark side, too, like we all have, and he drowned his sorrows and pain in alcohol, the only way he knew how to numb his feelings.

I often wonder how my Catherine will fare. She was only eight when her father left, and she hasn't seen him often over the years. She cut all ties with him a couple of years ago. Is he the example of a good husband in her eyes, or will she go for the complete opposite?

James was a good father. Something I loved about him was the fact that he took time to play with my kids, too; he truly interacted with all three of them. A while ago, Catherine told me that James was more of a father to her than her own father ever was. James was in our lives for less than two years, yet still, he left an impression on her about how a father could be.

He was an overbearing father to his son, though; it was too much. He so wanted to make Jason happy that it bordered on overdoing everything.

We once had a heated discussion about James' parenting style. I was calm and tried to explain to him that maybe a bit less would be more, and James wasn't interested in hearing my advice. He screamed at me, saying just because Toni was such an absent father to my children didn't mean that he (James) was parenting his son in the wrong way. I, of course, just curled up and tried to hide from this outburst. All I wanted to say was that, while Toni was at one end of the fathering spectrum, James was totally at the other end, and something in the middle might be better.

I now know that James was also looking for love—to be loved—just like me. I sought it from him, and he sought it from his son.

So yes, fathers or father figures are very important for girls. I was single throughout Catherine's puberty, so she didn't have a father figure in her life then; neither did Mathew or Horatio, and I wonder how that might influence them.

I am not sure how the lack of a father figure will help or hinder my children on their paths. For a long while, I tried to be both father and mother to my children. I learned that I can only be a mother and that even as a mother, I didn't need to be perfect. All I ever needed to be was myself, Caroline, and that was perfect.

Fathers sometimes form a beautiful bond with their daughters; I feel a father-daughter relationship is so very special and sacred. I am thankful for all the amazing fathers in this world, who show their daughters and sons what real men can be like.

I hope that my sons will be great fathers and uncles one day. They had to work through the pain of growing up with Toni, and they've worked to heal their wounds. Their experiences will feed into the men—the fathers and uncles—they become. They've learned to be true to themselves and be who they truly are.

I tried to teach my children by being true to myself.

They experienced their dad's fathering when they were small children. Yes, they were still little when we lived together, and as they grew up, he became an absent father. They experienced James as a surrogate dad during the time we were together. They saw how he interacted with them and how he interacted with Jason, his own son.

I was happy that my kids had male teachers all along during their school years, as well as other good role models—most of them were fathers too, with their sons and daughters at the same school.

When we are children, things might look a bit different than they do when we see it from an adult perspective. I trust that my children will be able to make their own decisions about their father and his impact in their lives.

Even though James was my boyfriend for those years, he must have felt conflicted about his role with my children. One day, he was playing with my children, and, when he came inside, he told me that Toni should pay him. I was taken aback. I asked, "Pay you for playing with his kids?" He said yes, and I nearly laughed out loud. He was not a nanny—he was my boyfriend, and I know he had fun playing with my kids. Looking back, I think that he felt guilty for playing with my kids while his own son was at his mother's—maybe that's why he said it, or maybe he truly meant it. Either way, he shouldn't have felt like he was owed money for doing a good deed—for playing with his significant other's children—especially if he initiated it and had a good relationship with the children. How strange was this notion? I know red flags were flying up, and I ignored them back then.

Maybe nowadays, as we enter a new era—a new feminine era—new male role models will emerge, and my children might be well served by not having had a clear role model. They can be more adaptable to exploring a new way of fatherhood, a type of fatherhood with compassion, love, and caring at its center.

Back to my father ... I realized, when looking at old photos, that my father really did love me. Deep healing took place, and some more grief was released.

My father passed away 25 years ago. As I turn 50 this year, I have lived half my life with my father on the other side. I was able to experience his love, compassion, and deep understanding from my work with the light. My father went back to universal, unconditional love and without the restrictions of this earthly life, he is able to share his love—pure love—and I am finally able to receive it.

I hope Toni and James don't have to pass into the light to reconnect with love. I hope that they are able to experience love here on earth, too.

The more I heal my relationships with my father, Toni, and James, the more I am healing my children's relationships with the men in their lives as well.

I'm sending love to all the men of this world. You are needed. Thank you, fathers, for sharing your love with your children, especially with your daughters. Thank you for being the men they can truly love.

How is your relationship with your father?

Wisdom From The Heart

Healing the father wound is truly amazing. As you work to heal your own father wound, you heal the father wound for your children too.

So sit quietly.

Breathe in deeply.

Connect with your father in a moment when he showed you love.

Let that moment come to you, maybe you can remember a photo of happy times or create a memory for yourself in your mind of a time when your father showed you love.

Just be in this moment.

Greet your father.

Tell him how much you love him.

Hug him.

And allow the love from your father flow to you.

Listen what he has to say to you (it might come in words, or a sense).

Allow the unconditional love to flow to you.

Connect deeper.

See a beautiful pink light connect your heart with the heart of your father.

And let that light shine brightly, clearing all the hurt and pain and feelings of being unloved.

Let that light shine love brightly.

Connect your love from your heart to the heart of your father.

Let that love travel from you to him and back to you.

See the waves washing to your shore and washing to his shore.

Feel that love.

Be that love.

Look your father in the eye

And tell him I love you.

See the love in your eyes.

Maybe hear him say he loves you.

Feel the love he shares with you

And know that your father loves you always and always will.

Breathe in that love.

Feel the connection.

Say thank you to your father.

And come back to the here and now.

Connecting to love is easy.

In meditation, we can connect to the higher self of a person, and the higher self is all about love.

Your father loved you, whether he was able to show it or not.

BIRTHDAYS

How important are birthdays and celebrations?

I was never good at celebrating myself, probably because I never felt good enough. Still, there were occasions I celebrated, like the time I had hung all the new prints I ordered, and I invited my friends over for a drink and 'art show'. It felt so good to celebrate the new me, the one that knew what kind of pictures she loved to have on her walls.

There was my 40th birthday, the summer after my marriage imploded. I remember fondly, having all my friends over in my house for an Apéritive (drinks and nibbles). I remember being there, surrounded by amazing, friendly, loving people who came to me to celebrate with me. That was a fabulous day.

This year, I will turn 50, and yes, I finally know how I would love to celebrate my birthday. I plan on celebrating in the mountains, in nature, with a hike with my children and my dog. Yes, I'll probably invite my mom, and my aunt and family will be there, too. We'll enjoy a wonderful day in nature and a good dinner in the evening. We'll celebrate half a century of *Caroline*. This feels good to me. Later, on a weekend date following my birthday, I will invite friends over for a get-together. It is always wonderful to celebrate, whether the celebration focuses on a birthday or something else entirely.

I also learnt that it is important to celebrate achievements. My first book won an award, and I did not truly honor it. I was happy—humbled, honored, and amazed—but I did not really have a celebration of any sort.

I didn't celebrate giving birth to my gorgeous children, either. Of course, I was happy that my children were healthy and had finally arrived in the world and I could hold them in my arms and see them. Even though I did acknowledge what I went through in birthing, I didn't really take time to honor the birthing ritual, the ritual of becoming a mom, entering motherhood. This is not something that is done in our western society, and there is often not much support for mothers in our society. I learned that there are traditions in other cultures where the community members bring food and help mothers who have just given birth, so they can focus on taking care of their newborn babies. Mothers in these societies are more fully supported.

Support is something that is missing in our lives nowadays. There is no community for many people. Often, we move far away from our families and have to do everything all on our own. We just do it. We keep going and that leaves little time for celebrations or rituals, little time to take a break and acknowledge our hard work and ourselves.

Like the example of celebrating motherhood: Having a child is such a major change in our lives, and we just try to keep on going, as if nothing truly monumental just happened. We often feel like we need to go back to how things were before—like our bodies have to slim down again to our pre-natal figures. Models and society's expectations put a lot of pressure on women about this.

Why can't we celebrate our bodies for the amazing miracles they produced? Our bodies grew other human beings, nurtured those babies for nine months and then gave birth, pushing those babies out into the world. This is amazing in itself! Plus, our bodies are able to feed babies for the first months. Why, oh why do we feel the need for our bodies to go right back to the way they were before we got pregnant, as if nothing happened?

I know Toni pressured me into slimming down after I had Horatio, with comments like, "Why can't you lose weight? Why are you still so chubby? Isn't it time to lose the baby weight?" and so on.

Of course, I managed to lose the weight eventually, though I missed out on giving love to my body, missed out on celebrating the wonders this body was capable of—not once, not twice, but three times. My body gave me the greatest gifts ever, three amazing, wonderful, gorgeous children. I should have taken the time to celebrate. Yes, I know women around the world give birth, still it is something extraordinary and so worth celebrating and honoring women for.

One time, when I posted about my child's birthday, one friend commented, "Happy Birthing Day!" At first

I thought she misspelled happy birthday, and then it hit me: Yes, she congratulated my body and me for birthing my child. Indeed, celebrating our children's birthdays are also celebrations of the birthing process we went through. My fabulous friend always brought flowers to Horatio's birthday celebrations—gorgeous smelling wild roses—always for me—the mother who gave birth to her son that day.

So celebrating is very important. It is an acknowledgment of who we are and how far we have come. It is a celebration of love for ourselves.

Nowadays, I realize how important it is to celebrate our mothers, too. I thank my mom for giving birth to me. It never occurred to me as a child or as a young woman—or even as a young mother—that when I celebrate my birthday, my mom is also celebrating birthing me. As I was the oldest, she is also celebrating the rite of passage into motherhood with my birth.

Talking about birthdays ... I remember my 41st birthday. My mom was with us, and James was there, too. We prepared breakfast, and he got a call from his son, who told him that he missed him. James dashed out of the house, telling us he was going to get his son. We waited for him to return. We added an extra plate so that Jason could join us and we waited, till we eventually started eating our breakfast.

James never called and returned very late that day. He had no idea we were waiting and didn't understand why I was upset as he didn't feel like he did anything wrong. I wanted to celebrate my birthday with him, and he, of course, went to get his son. I felt like he had abandoned me. He could have called and told me that he wouldn't return. It seemed as if he originally planned to be back. He said he would. Giving me a call would have been the least he could do. So celebrating my birthday that year did not go as planned.

Nowadays, I celebrate my birthday MY WAY. Last year, for the very first time, I did exactly what I wanted on my birthday. My kids and I went on a boat ride and to a beautiful city of roses. We had lunch there, and enjoyed a wonderful day together. I let go of having to celebrate with my sisters or my mom; I chose to celebrate only with my kids, doing what I love. I love being on the lake on a boat; it is so soothing and the perfect way to celebrate my birthday. I finally had the birthday of my dreams. It felt good. Celebrating my birthday like this felt freeing and it was perfect. The day was so nice that I didn't even mind when my kids fought like children sometimes do!

What is your fondest birthday memory?

Wisdom From The Heart

Sit somewhere quietly.

Look back over your shoulder and
See how far you have come.
Embrace all your experiences,
And feel proud of yourself.
Celebrate yourself and your life by acknowledging how far you have come.
Bow to yourself and all you have accomplished.

Oftentimes, we only look forward and how far we still have to go.
Taking time to look back and acknowledge how far we have already come is life changing.

WAITING FOR LOVE

Are you still waiting for the love of your life?

Right now I am single, so, yes, in a way, I'd love to meet my soul mate, but I am not waiting around per se.

What does a soul mate mean to me? It means meeting a man I can relate to in my heart, body, mind, soul and spirit. Maybe you have heard of the term Twin Flame, for me it is more like meeting a long lost friend, someone you feel instantly close to, someone with whom there is a mutual understanding and respect, someone you have spent past lives with, someone you know on a soul level, without having met them in this life, you feel you know each other already. A soul mate for me means a man I can exchange great and profound discussions with, a man I experience a wonderful passion with, someone I love deeply truly and who loves me deeply and truly for who I am, someone who is true to himself and is free to come on this wonderful journey with me called a relationship, where we learn so much more about ourselves than we ever could on our own. A journey we promise to walk together and grow together. I know this soul mate to be out there and we will meet at the perfect time.

You see, you can sit around and wait for love, or you can be actively engaged in love. You can be the love of your life and feel the love in your life while you are single.

I know many of us are always waiting for the perfect day, the perfect love, the perfect job, the perfect vacation. Many people are waiting for the day they can finally live. "Once I have this job," they think. "Once I have this kind of money, once I have this car, once I … then I can do this or that, then I can finally be enough."

We are living in *this* moment, right here right now. We can embrace all that we are, or we can wait to feel good once we have found our soul mates.

I am love, I feel loved, and I love others here and now. I don't need a soul mate to feel loved. I've done that before—waited until someone else loved me before I felt love. I was needy for love, and I only felt loved when I was in a relationship.

Now I know better. Now I know I am love and I can feel that love, even as a single woman. I am myself as much as possible, even when I am in a new relationship.

Yes, I still have a tiny bit of fear that I might give myself up again in my next romantic relationship. I still feel like I might fall back into old habits, like needing to please my partner, to give myself up to make my partner happy, and I also fear another failed relationship. I know I am a 'burned child,' so I fear the fire. I am continually working on healing this feeling and releasing it on new levels. It takes time, patience, compassion, and yes, it also takes a lot of love.

I don't chase after love. I deeply trust that I will meet my soul mate, and I trust the Universe to deliver him at the perfect time.

I also know deep down that I am ready for a healthy relationship, and that I won't take crap any longer. I feel more worthy now than I did when I was with James and way more than when I was with Toni.

I am also happily single. That means, if a new relationship does not work out, I know that I can survive alone. I did not have that wisdom eight years ago when I desperately clung to James and the dysfunctional relationship we had. Back then, I preferred to be in a relationship instead of being single. Now my mantra is very much different: I'd rather be on my own than with the wrong man.

So no, I am not waiting for love. I _am_ love right here and right now.

I also know that a soul mate relationship is not all bliss and glitter, and that I will grow even more in a new relationship. So much healing will be mirrored, and so much will come up to the surface by being in a relationship again, especially after eight years of being single.

So yes, I am waiting for a soul mate, not in the way that feels like I will only be happy once I have finally found him or he has found me, and not in a way that has me sitting around, waiting. On the contrary, I am not looking on any partnership sites, nor am I frequenting any bars; I am doing inner work. I am healing my heart, opening up, and embracing the possibilities of a beautiful new romantic relationship. And yes, I trust the Universe and I listen to my intuition more now that I have learned to trust my gut.

The past has brought me to this moment, so I am grateful for all of my experiences, without which I would not be in this place.

I am done with waiting for something or someone to come along in my life to make me happy. I am actively being Caroline as best as I can, knowing that a future romantic partner would be working on being the best version of himself, too.

I am shedding layers of pain and worry and healing myself as I go. I am learning to embrace Caroline more and more each day.

What are you waiting for?

Wisdom From The Heart

There is no better time than now.

You have all you need already within.

The best time to plant an oak tree was 25 years ago; the second best time is today.

What are you waiting for? Go pursue your dreams now!

Follow your bliss.

Follow your heart.

You are so ready.

These are just a couple of reminders that have helped me along my journey. I hope they inspire you too.

Maybe write them down on post-it notes and hang them around your home, as loving reminders for yourself.

TRUST IN LOVE

How can we trust in love?

I know we always fear that if we open our hearts, we're going to get hurt. We'd prefer to keep everyone at a safe distance and put up our armor so we won't end up suffering.

This attitude is totally understandable, as we've been all hurt before, but it is not a good way to go through life. Shutting ourselves down to the possibility of being hurt also shuts us down from experiencing joy and love. We end up feeling like we're living in a grey world when we could be living in a gorgeously bright and colorful world.

Yes, opening our hearts and feeling the flow of love again takes trust and courage. We have to unlearn everything we believe is true, and release pain and heartache so we can come back to love and our hearts.

Many of us only trust our thinking-brains and don't feel like we can truly follow our hearts because they will only lead us astray. You could point the finger at me, and telling me that I followed my heart, and was led astray during my relationships Toni and James. You could say that I ended up with my heart broken because I followed my heart. You could argue that the heart is stupid.

Yes, I trusted too much, but I also did not listen to or follow my intuition.

Yes, I followed my heart in the beginning of the relationships, but I also shut it down and kept going toward the end. It was actually my intellect that wanted to reason, to silence my heart and my intuition.

And yes, I closed down my heart, too. After my relationships with Toni and James, I felt like I couldn't take it anymore. I did not want to feel anything any more, and I did not want to be hurt again.

I had so wanted to stay in those unhealthy relationships—to make them work—that I didn't listen to my internal nudges, my heart, or my intuition. I was fixated on being in a relationship or making my marriage work, even though it had already ended years before.

I was not let down by my heart or by men; I was let down by myself because I tried to hold on to something that was over or wasn't making me happy to begin with.

I still hear my mom telling me all men are bad, and we can't trust men. Can't we? Why not? Just because I dated two bad apples, does not mean that all men are bad.

Deep down in me, I still have hope—hope for humanity, hope for love, and hope for myself.

Yes, we can trust in love. Love exists, and love is our true essence. Everyone on the earth experiences love differently, even within different relationships in their own lives.

We can experience what love is by surrendering, by allowing ourselves to trust the Universe, and by trusting our intuition and internal nudges. By embracing all we are, and by truly loving without expectations, we open ourselves to feeling true love.

I remember a moment when I felt the Universal love. In my darkest hour, I had a sign from the Universe and a reassurance about love.

I was at my wits' end. My relationship with James just disintegrated. I had money problems, as Toni just single-handedly lowered my alimony payments, and I had debts piled up from my move. (I shared this story in more detail in my first book, *Conversations With Me*.) I felt lonely, I felt abused, and I did not know how to keep going.

I threw myself on my bed, and I cried and cried. I was just exhausted and overwhelmed by everything. I remember lying on my belly, and crying into my hands.

Then all of a sudden I 'saw'—more like feeling and seeing with my inner eyes—like from the perspective of an outside observer—the sky opening up and a large hand surrounded by yellow light coming down from the heavens and touching me on my back. It was amazing! The feeling it left was so reassuring and deeply loving. It felt like the hand of God had come down to me, to caress me, to let me know that everything would be all right, to help me through this, to give me trust, and to reassure me.

I will never forget this moment. I was so in awe that the Universe had come to me and told me everything is going to be all right. It was the light I needed in my moment of despair, the light that guided me out of the darkest of tunnels, the light that ignited the light in my heart again, the light that ignited my love for my life and myself again.

Yes, I learned to trust in love again, and so can you.

Love is something we can all connect to each and every day. We can reconnect with our hearts and feel the love from within. We can also reconnect with Mother Earth and feel her nurturing, motherly love. We can reconnect with the Universe and feel that fatherly, protective all-encompassing love again.

Sometimes we just need a reminder of the profound love we came from—the reassurance we are still love— in order to know to trust love again.

So yes, I trust my love within me. I trust my heart and my intuition. I also trust Mother Earth to nurture me, and the Universe to lovingly protect and guide me.

I trust in love.

Do you trust in love?

Wisdom From The Heart

We can all light a candle and shine. We can let the light shine on our darkest fears, and bring light to ourselves in our sorrow.

Sit somewhere quietly.

Breathe in deeply,

deep down into your belly.

Close your eyes.

Imagine you are holding a candle.

Ask the Angels and the Universe to light your candle.

Allow your candle to be lit, and shine bright.

See your candle shining brighter and brighter

Now take your candle and bring it towards your fears.

Let the candle illuminate your fears.

Let the candle set your fears free.

Spread some love and compassion to your fears.

Now shine your light on your sorrows.

Allow your sorrows to soak up the light and warmth of the candle, and be lightened by its shine.

Look at the candle.

Breathe in the gorgeous light,

The warmth the love it brings.

Then bring that candle into your heart.

Ignite your heart with all the love there is.

Let your heart shine bright and light.

Shine that light into your whole body.

And shine that light into the world.

Remember you are love.

Take a deep breath.

Breathe in the love.

And come back to the here and now.

You are love and you can bring the light to anything that worries you. Practice bringing light to all areas of your life.

WINE

What wine do you love?

I've had on an on and off love affair with wine. You see, Toni loved wine, and we often shared a bottle of wine at dinner.

I loved wine, sometimes a bit too much. I now know a bit about drowning one's sorrows and pain, and I also know I wanted that gaping hole of feeling unloved to vanish. I did not want to face reality—the fact that I was in a loveless marriage—and I did not want to face the consequences of my reality.

I also liked beer, though Toni felt beer was more a pub drink. He loathed beer, so I only drank beer when I was out with friends, never at home.

After Toni left, I had a glass of wine sometimes in the evening. Drinking alone didn't feel right though, and I did not feel like I had anything to celebrate by myself. Plus, it had been heartbreaking for my marriage to end, and somehow I didn't feel the need to drown that pain by drinking wine. I knew a new chapter had started, and I wanted to do things differently. Drinking wine reminded me too much of my life with Toni.

So when James came into my life and he loved beer, I naturally switched over to drinking beer instead of wine. I like beer. I learned about Weissbier and different kind of beers, too. Sometimes we had a glass of wine, together, but it wasn't the same.

Toni had accumulated a lot of wine over the years, and he took his part with him when he left. Even after Toni took all the wine he wanted with him, I still had plenty left in the cellar.

One day, James talked me into giving him two boxes of wine for 'safekeeping'. I remember feeling odd about giving the wine to him. He told me they would be safe at his workplace; they had a good cellar, and he could put them there so Toni could not get to them. Toni could not get to the wine anyway, as I had ordered him to give me back the key to the house. Somehow, despite my nagging doubts, I let James talk me into giving him two boxes of wine—good wine.

Yes, you guessed it. I never saw that wine again. James wouldn't even bring me the boxes of wine when he was packing his things at my house. It seems that, all along, he planned on having the wine for himself.

It seems like he wanted my wine, but I wonder if he ever wanted me.

I remember James telling me that he'd had some Gaia Wine, but his wife drank it all. Somehow, he reasoned, it was good that the Universe provides and always brings things back. He did not use the word, *Universe*, as he was not a spiritual person. He was very good at telling me what I wanted to hear, though, suggesting that we were meant to be because of some wine. So he thought that he was meant to receive the wine from me? Did he think that because his wine was gone, he had a way to get the wine back through me? It was a twisted way of thinking, and back then I was still so blinded by love that I made excuses for him. I should have been listening to my heart—I know that now.

I did not drink much alcohol after James was gone. I was done numbing my pain. I was ready to face my feelings, and I was ready to take an inward journey—a journey to reconnect to the love within myself.

Over the years, I gave bottles of wine away. I used them for payment. I used wine as gifts for friends and relatives, as I still had plenty.

Now, since we've moved into our new place, I've started to have a glass of wine again every now and then, and I'm coming back to a place where I like wine again. I still have a nagging resentment towards James for taking two boxes of expensive wine away from me. It's a wine I would LOVE to drink now, a wine I would cherish and savor these days. I am kind of angry with myself for falling into his trap. I know my anger is a sign of needing to do a little more healing to bring myself back to love again.

I never said I was perfect, did I?

Isn't it funny that, when I had an abundance of wine but I preferred beer, I did not treasure the wine as much? Now that I have only a couple of bottles of wine left, I prefer wine over beer.

What does that show us? It shows me that we should cherish everything we have—all parts of us—the wine lover and the beer lover, equally. We can appreciate one bottle of wine just as easily as we can cherish 1,000 bottles. It doesn't matter how much or little we have of something, as long as we feel grateful for it.

And yes, I know what wine I like now. I really like white wine. I love the grapes of Pinot Grigio the best. I also like red wine, a pure wine coming from one sort of grapes—not a mixture—mostly Italian, and yes, I still enjoy a refreshing beer or the mix we call Panache or Radler, which is a mixture of beer and lemon-lime soda. I also love a glass of Prosecco or bubbly. I also enjoy a good glass of Aperol Spritz with friends or by myself.

Deep down, I still fear my genes might carry the trait of alcoholism. I worried that I might have inherited the alcoholic gene from my father, until I realized that he was deeply unhappy and had no other way to numb his pain. I saw the same pattern happening in myself in the past, but I've found other ways to deal with my feelings.

Nowadays, after having gone through so much, after learning so much about myself and growing in love, I am happy about who I am—all of me—so there's no need for me to numb any pain anymore. While I might sometimes feel the need to have a glass of wine to soothe myself, I have learned other ways of releasing stress, too, and ways to prevent it. I look after myself better and take quiet breaks and self-care periods throughout each day.

So yes, I enjoy a glass of wine. I know which wines I like, and finally, I don't look for specific names on the labels, but more for the smell in my nose and the taste on my tongue, and yes, I can spot a corky wine very well, which makes me proud.

I remember one evening years ago, we were at a dinner at a friends' house with some wine lovers, and I could not drink the wine because it was corky, and no one realized it but me. I still have to smile, thinking about all those men who were talking about wine, and feeling so sophisticated, yet they could not even smell the cork in the glass in front of them?

You might wonder why a spiritual person—a healer of hearts—would drink alcohol, and whether I can call myself spiritual and a healer while doing so.

"Why not?" I ask you.

We can be spiritual and have coffee, drink a glass of wine, eat meat, and be the best healers, too. One doesn't exclude the other.

We are humans, and we are spiritual, and we are perfect just the way we are.

I know the spiritual community can be very judgmental, and that is the way for some. I have learned to embrace myself for who I truly am, and by feeling compassion and understanding for myself, I learned to release judgment. I am more accepting of others because I accept myself. So yes, we are all spiritual, and we are all human, we are all perfect, and we are all divine. We can all do what is best for ourselves, no matter what that looks like. If you feel called to abstain from alcohol, good for you. If you are called to eat only vegan foods, that's perfect. I am happy you know what is good for you.

How do you like your wine or food?

Wisdom From The Heart

Sometimes the things we crave can be signs of what we want in life.

For example, when I crave chocolate, I know I am actually craving love, so I take extra time to add some self-love to my routine.

When I crave a beer, I know I am actually looking for companionship, so I call friends and organize a get together.

Wine, I know, is a sign for me to have some down time.

While it is OK to enjoy a glass or two in an evening, overdoing it isn't good.

Of course, if you feel that you have more severe issues with alcohol or compulsive eating, you should seek out help from a licensed therapist or support group that deals with overeating or alcoholism.

We can also ask the food or drink whether it is good for us.

You can hold up your arm and put the food or drink you want to know about in your hand and ask yourself, "Is this good for me and my body right now?"

If your hand feels heavy and falls down, it is a sign of what you are asking about not being good.

If it feels light and stable, then you can enjoy!

And remember, we all have cravings and we all sometimes overindulge, that is OK, too. Try not to beat yourself up over it. Be compassionate toward yourself. If, however, you feel like you need to indulge every day, maybe it is time to adjust routine, and implement more breaks and self-care into your days, so you feel less of a need to indulge at the end of each day.

♥

I AM NOT WORTHY

How can you make yourself feel worthy?

That is an excellent question. I know for most of my life I felt profoundly unworthy. So simply saying, "I am worthy," or having someone tell me that I was worthy didn't truly help.

There were enough people who told me, "Of course, you are worthy. What do you think? You have three kids, and you exist, so you are worthy," and things like that, but it never resonated. I just thought to myself, "Yeah you can talk. Keep on talking—you have no idea."

They probably didn't understand how unworthy I felt. I did not only feel undeserving, I also had a deep feeling of self-loathing. I was unhappy with myself; I was unhappy with my body, shape, and form; I was unhappy with who I was—about the fact that I was highly sensitive and I felt like I was a complete failure.

I was unworthy as a wife. I was unworthy as a mom, because I was not perfect enough, because I lost my temper every now and then, and because I could not simply be happy. I could not be content with the lot I had in my life. Why couldn't I just be happy about being married and happy about having my three beautiful children? Why, oh why, did I fancy a romantic love a passionate love—a savior and a knight in shining armor who would come to my rescue and make everything bright, shiny, and loving from the time I met him?

I didn't realize back then that I am *my own* knight in shining armor, that only I can rescue myself, and that I actually did not need rescuing after all. All I ever needed to do was to connect with myself; I had everything I needed already in me. Everything I longed for was already in my heart. I had the wisdom, the love, the compassion, and yes, the knowledge that everything was there, waiting for me.

I only needed to unlock the door to my heart.

Easier said than done, right?

I had locked my door to my heart so tight and then I threw away the key.

Looking back, I now see that feeling unworthy had become my way of being.

In my mind, I deserved every negative thing that was said to me, every word I felt was mumbled behind my back, everything that happened to me, because I wasn't good enough, even though feeling unworthy and being treated poorly became a cycle.

What if all that was said and all that had happened actually happened for my benefit, not to keep me down, but to help me find my way?

What if, by Toni always talking down to me, he actually stirred that tiny ember of self-worth that was still smoldering in the ashes?

What if the Universe encouraged Toni to keep stirring, till I finally had enough to stand up and tell him to go and "*&%ç himself?

What if James was actually there to make me feel so used, unloved, and lonely that I was finally able to go deep within and reconnect with the tiny bit of love that I held on to within myself?

What if it was all meant to be?

Of course, I know it was all meant to be. Often our greatest hardships turn out to be our biggest blessings later on. Yes, our problems can be blessings in disguise.

Often, the people who are struggling with self-worth and who loathe themselves with a passion can end up feeling the most profound compassion and the deepest love for themselves.

Sitting here, writing these words, touches my heart. I have tears in my eyes, as the words ring so true. I feel so much compassion for the experiences I went through and for myself. I feel a deep sense of nurturing and beautiful love for myself, which I never thought would be possible.

So how, you might ask, was I able to not only find the key to my heart, but how was I also able to open the heavy door that blocked me from my own love?

I realized that I had the key all along; our keys can never be lost.

Opening the door to my heart again was as easy as waving a feather.

Once we understand how hard it is to keep our hearts blocked, once we start letting go of all that we thought we needed to be, the door just collapses by itself. We might feel a bit intimidated, sensitive, or tearful by releasing it all, and yes, we might also feel amazed, deeply humbled, and touched by our own love.

The surprising part is that opening our hearts is so easy, simple, and pure.

By allowing my feelings—all of my feelings—to come up, by allowing myself to experience life as deeply as I was always meant to, I was opening my heart. Rest assured, it is not painful to open our hearts, not as painful as it was when we closed our hearts so we wouldn't be hurt again.

By allowing ourselves to come back to the essence of feelings, embracing our emotions, and allowing our energies to flow freely, we are coming back to ourselves, to being our own truth, and embracing the human beings we are. Anything else is a lie—an act.

Yes, I heard that I should put my mind over matter so many times that it numbed me. It was another way of saying I was not good enough. I tried to shove my feelings aside, until I realized we humans are meant to have feelings, and that the feelings are part of living a full and healthy life.

Suppressing or hiding parts of ourselves hinders us from being true to ourselves.

Are you ready to embrace all of you—to accept your body, your feelings, and your thoughts? I am asking you, "Are you ready to love and accept the essence of your soul?"

Are you ready to embrace it by embracing all your past experiences, and by embracing all that you are, more and more each day?

Yes, you will need to tap into your courage, into your heart, into you truest being and your soul. It will be a journey, but it will be so worth it! Only when you can tap into your heart and the essence of your being can you truly express who you are and live a deeply fulfilled life—the life you came here to lead. This is the life the Universe deemed us worthy of.

By connecting to our hearts, we are finally fulfilling the role we came here to play on this earth, and yes, we are so worthy of doing this.

I know you are ready to unlock your heart and live the role the Universe assigned you. Do you know it, too?

Wisdom From The Heart

Do you know how hard it is to hold on?

Imagine yourself on a boat on a river. You are holding on to a branch, as you want to stay where you are.

The boat wants to float further down the river, but you are holding on tight to the branch of that tree.

Do you feel your arm starting to hurt from holding on, from going against the river, the flow?

Do you realize how truly tiring holding on is?

Now imagine yourself letting go, and just sitting in your gorgeous little boat.

Observe the landscape going by.

Allow your boat and your life to go with the flow in the river of life.

Allow your boat to naturally go ashore at a landing and take your time to go out and explore.

And when you are ready, come back to your boat and let the stream of life take you to your next destination.

Promise yourself that you will no longer hold on to things that are not meant to be.

Promise yourself that you will allow yourself to go with the flow

And keep flowing.

Trust what was meant to be will always be,

And what no longer serves you will flow away.

The only constant in our lives is change.

Be happy, smile, and embrace all the new coming your way.

UNIFYING LOVE

Does love unite?

Oh, absolutely! Love is the ribbon that holds it all together. Love is the energy that makes people understand that we are all equal.

Love it our essence—our true nature—whether we are male, female; black, white or Asian; baby, teenager or grown adult; young or old. We are all love. Being love goes even further: whether a being is human, animals, or plant, love is its life form.

Love unites us, where fear divides us.

Love understands us, where language might be a barrier.

Love invites us, where cultures might feel foreign.

Love simply is, and through loving eyes, we see we are all equals in the love of the Creator. We are only different in the ways we express our lives.

You know, I had a tough time embracing the masculine energy within me. Yes, I knew about yin and yang energies, but I was so much more aligned with the feminine side of myself. I also feared the masculine might be overpowering. I had some experiences with males in my life that might have influenced my feelings about male energy.

Many of us might have also lived past lives in which we were burnt at the stake, or where we were punished for being who we were, so a deep fear of male or church oppression is still within us.

For example, the word power had such a negative energy for me. I did not want to feel powerful. I did not want to become the oppressor. I shied away from my own power too, until I realized I could be powerful in my very own way.

When I hold a meditation or a healing session, I am powerful. I am so deeply grounded with Mother Earth, standing tall and proud, so connected to the Universe, and so deeply supported as an open channel. Yes, that is powerful to me—it is my own way of being powerful.

How can you embrace your own unique power?

We all have images in our heads of how females have to be or males should act. We often forget that we all have both feminine and masculine energy in us and that the balance is key.

When women push aside their male energy like I did, we sometimes lack the ability to manifest, or we lack the energy to bring our visions and love into reality.

When we suppress our female energy, we forget to nurture, we forget that we are all one, and we forget to receive in a loving way.

When I look at the world now, I see we could create a better world if we would all connect to the love within ourselves, and share from a loving, caring place.

I also shied away from the feminism in the past. I never liked the word or the energy that seemed to state that woman are better than men, or have to prove we are somehow better.

We are not better and we are not superior. We are women, and we are equal to men. The world needs both; it needs a balance of the energies. It was never about competition. It was always about integrating, about understanding, about being truthful.

Yes, we need brilliant analytical thinkers, both male and female.

We need leaders, both female and male.

We need nurturer and caregivers, both male and female.

We need you, and me, and all of us.

Love is the puzzle that unites us all. Love is the bridge between countries, languages, and continents. Love is also the compassion between men and women, families and communities. Love is what makes the world go round.

I have finally allowed myself to embrace my male energies, too. I have an even deeper understanding of being human and being a woman. I feel whole.

By embracing all of ourselves, we embrace the entire world.

By understanding ourselves, we can understand the world.

By loving ourselves, we love the entire world

By being loving towards ourselves, we can finally love everyone on the planet.

After years of being ruled by male energy, we are entering a more feminine energy at the moment. What does that mean?

Does that mean that women have finally the say?

Not really. It means that we allow more compassion, nurturing, and loving into our lives, whether we are women or men. It means that we use the base of compassion and nurturing to influence our communities and societies.

This does not mean that all men are bad or that masculine energy is negative energy, not at all. I am all for integration of the different types of energies for love. The key is that, when we all allow more of the feminine energy into our beings, we also allow more male energy into our lives. Women who were suppressed or feared male energy will be able to open up to a loving male energy; they will understand that masculine energy is not about suppression at all.

We all need both masculine and feminine energy, the characteristics that go with both types. The whole world needs both. We need to learn to balance and unify the two energies.

Let's open our eyes and hearts to everything that is around us. Embrace all that is, and allow love to unify our planet and our Universe. We need Mother Earth Energy and Father Sky Energy: Nurturing Mother Earth and Protective and Masculine Universal Energy.

We know:

Love heals everything.

Love conquers everything.

Love unites everything.

We are in desperate need of unifying love now.

Are you ready to unify?

Wisdom From The Heart

See a circle everywhere you go. Imagine the Ying and Yang sign, perfectly embracing both energies.

Breathe in deeply.

Breathe in yin and yang energy.

Breathe it into every cell of your body.

Embrace both masculine and feminine energy.

Feel the unifying love wander through your body

from toe to head and from head to toe.

Allow that unifying love to flow out of every pore of your body

And surround yourself with unifying love.

Unify in yourself.

Unify outside of yourself.

Bring unity to this world.

Be a wonderful example of unifying love.

EPILOGUE

So where are you now?

That's a good question. I am in a wonderful place. I love my life. I feel deep compassion for myself. I am embracing all that is coming my way, and I trust—I have a deep trust in the Universe and in myself.

We recently moved into a smaller flat that is full of light and easier for me to maintain. It even has a little garden patch so that we can sit outside with our animals and enjoy the fresh air.

I feel so good about my life and myself. I have close relationships with all my three children. The boys still live at home and my daughter is abroad at university. We often chat via video chat, and she comes home for her breaks.

I am deeply grateful for my children, my life, and all of my experiences.

Looking back now, I see how far I have come, and I am amazed, proud of my journey and myself. Every day, I feel a more profound understanding, broader compassion, and more authentic love for myself. I feel my heart opening and I allow myself to be more and more open and full of love each day.

Writing these stories has helped me become even more loving towards myself. Writing is healing for me.

I hope reading my stories helps you heal, too.

You might wonder how Toni and James are these days.

Toni is no longer a part of our lives. I have to deal with his unpleasant attitude when I send him bills for extra costs for the children. His bullying emails sometimes still hurt me, so I take a breath and treasure myself even more after I read his messages. I embrace my sensitivity, my feelings. I take a step back and see Toni from an outside perspective and then I am fine, happy to be me, and happy that he is no longer part of my life.

James left eight years ago, and I had not heard anything at all from him until recently, when he sent me a text inquiring how I was doing. At first, I wasn't even sure of who sent the message. I considered writing back, and then I asked myself, "Do I still have parts to heal? Do I need to write back?" I got a clear no and no. I know it was the Universe sending me a sign that it was time to write this book. I've shared the stories of James and how much he has helped me bring myself back to love after he left. I healed more parts of feeling used by him, making peace with all that was. I found compassion to who I was back then.

I have grown so much over the last couple of years, and distant friends feel like they don't know me anymore. I sometimes smile and think, "You never knew me. You never knew the person I was deep down." My close friends and family are happy for me, and my aunt recently told me that she is so happy to see her Caroline again, the one she knows from childhood, the Caroline I always was. Being Caroline is the best part of my healing for me.

Each day we grow, each day we can become more loving, and each day brings new opportunities for growth, acceptance, and self-love.

I am happy where I am, with who I am, and with the person I've become.

I wish you happiness and love in all areas of your life, too.

FINAL WISDOM FROM THE HEART

I recently read that in Greek there were 6 words for love.

I found this intriguing.

Eros
Sexual passion and desire

Philia
Deep loyalty to friends

Ludus
Playful love

Agape
Love for everyone

Pragma
Love developed over time

Philautia
Taking care of the self

There is also a 7th word for love

Storge
Familial Love

I absolutely love these, and I hope you can dive into each one of them on a daily basis.

I love you.

ACKNOWLEDGEMENT

I would love to take a minute to thank:

My parents

My sisters

My friends

All the teachers in my life

My partners

Toni and James, without whom I would not be where I am now.

And I'd love to give thanks to myself for being able to walk through life, experience it fully, and for taking one step after another, even during the times I felt like I was down and could not go on any longer.

And most of all, I want to say thank you to my three gorgeous children, who have shown me what love is all about and are my greatest teachers, always. Thank you. I love you so very much.

I thank Love.

Thank you for showing what you are, how true you are, and how blissful you can be.

Thank you for showing me that I am love, that we are all love.

I thank the Universe, Mother Earth, and all the spiritual beings who have helped me along, who shared their love with me and helped me see myself for who I am.

I thank you, too, my dear reader, for reading this book and coming on this journey to love with me.

♥

SPECIAL THANKS GO TO

Susan Ellis-Saller

Thank you, Sue, for being the most amazing editor, for using your magic wand and transforming my words into even more love.

Thank you for making my stories easier to read and to understand. Thanks for clarifying my messages, so they come from my heart and reach the hearts of the readers.

Thank you for all your insights and feedback.

Thank you for your magic and for being a dear friend.

Sean Patrick

Thank you, Sean, for being a most fabulous publisher, for guiding me through these chapters, for giving me insightful and encouraging feedback, and yes, for helping me share the love with this world.

Thank you for being you and sharing your love of words. You are the best publisher I could have and thank you for being a wonderful friend, too.

Karen Mills-Alston

Thank you, Karen, for taking the time to read this book and for writing a heartfelt foreword.

I had tears in my eyes when I read your beautiful words. I was deeply touched

Thank you for your time, your insight, and your love. You are a wonderful friend. I feel deeply blessed knowing you.

Monica Maurer and Paula Smeaton

Thank you, Monica and Paula, for being amazing photographers and capturing my essence so well. I never liked having pictures taken or posing for photos. You both made it so much fun, either as an appointed photo shoot or an impromptu photo session.

I am honored to use your work on the cover of my book. Thank you for being able to capture my essence so truly.

ENDORSEMENTS

Caroline is a wonderful soul and her work to bring people back into flow with their hearts is a special gift. She is an inspiration and her books not only offer hope, but provide simple steps to get back into 'heart flow'.

Janet Groom
Writer/Author & Book Coach
JanetGroom.com

As someone who's often found it difficult to love and find her way to her heart and self, it was first very uncomfortable getting to know Caroline, but when you do, a whole new world opens up.

A world of love and healing. A world of appreciation and consideration. Empathy and understanding. Caroline is an incredible human being, mother, dog-lover and person and her compassion and fire to assist others in finding the love to themselves and those around them is infectious. Thank you for being you Caroline! I love you too!

Sashka Hanna Rappl
Brand Master & Business Strategist,
Author, Speaker
BrandSashka.com

Caroline Palmy is the presence of calm. Her soothing voice brings me to a centre of calm and whenever I hear it, I am instantly at peace. As a healer she is subtle but powerful, her heart flow healing sessions are a delight. Caroline is a loving presence that we could all do with more of in our lives.

Sam Livermore
Gladiator of Love
SamLivermore.com

Caroline Palmy is such a kind and beautiful warm-hearted deep soul. Her level of warmth and energy can only be obtained by facing and breaking through great struggle and challenge. She is able to take her experience, her journey, and her connection with the Divine to help her clients and the world to attain higher levels of peace, awareness, and connection. Caroline is one of those special souls who is here on Earth to bring us to a new beginning, a new awakening, and a higher level of consciousness.

Pete Cossaboon,
Healer/inspirational coach
PeteCossaboon.com

Caroline Palmy is a master memoirist. Her ability to speak to the human experience through the written word is phenomenal. She delivers ageless wisdom in a gentle and powerful way. She is truly one of a kind.

Sean Patrick
Director and founder of
That Guy's House
ThatGuysHouse.com

Caroline has such a gentle spirit. I've had the pleasure to be part of several healing circles she's given and each time it's as if I have taken a bath in warm water. She's got the most amazing way of calming and providing peace.

Leigh Daniel
Founder of Project Positive Change
ProjectPositiveChange.com

Caroline brings her joyful sparkle to everything she touches, I am blessed to call her my friend. When I met Caroline for the first time I was enveloped by her strong, nurturing love as though I was her long lost child - she is an incredibly powerful woman and she knew immediately that I was part of her family x Knowing Caroline is a soul connection x

Jodee Peevor
Founder of Lower House Events who
runs Jodee's Teepee Weekender for
soul-centred entrepreneurs
JodeePeevor.com

Caroline is one of the kindest, most loving women I have ever met. I am in awe of how far she has come on her self-love journey.

It is with great joy that I witness how much love and kindness Caroline has for herself and how much she genuinely loves and cares for others.

She is a powerful role model for anyone who longs to fill up their own well in order to overflow with love to support others and change the world.

I highly recommend Caroline and her beautiful work. She is the real deal and always shows up authentically and with such a loving heart.

Karina Ladet
Intuitive Channel & Mentor
KarinaLadet.com

Caroline is an extraordinary woman

Caroline Palmy is love

She embodies and infuses her work with her deep understanding of what it is to Love ourselves and others in today's world; the challenges of modern life and realities we move through. Caroline is a beautiful, courageous and gentle soul. She adeptly guides you down to path of love and the language of our souls, the tonic we seek, so we can love the life we live.

Adele Winkley
Small Business Coach and Intuitive
Energy Healer
ConceptToCreation.co.uk

I have had the pleasure of working with Caroline on a few occasions. Her energy is like a big warm hug, enveloping you, her voice is so calming, comforting and nurturing and her words are so wise. I had the privilege of listening to her talk and the way she connects to the heart is so beautiful!

Personally I found being in Caroline's company, we didn't need to talk, there was a comfortable inner knowing. The work she is doing is so important for the world right now, the shift in to self love and reconnecting to the heart is needed for us all to move forward.

Elizabeth Goddard
Soul Transformation Therapist • Soul Plan Reader • Reiki Master Teacher • Author - Finding Lily
ReviveYourSoul.co.uk

I have known Caroline for a number of years now, and every time I speak with her what comes shining through is the light of her love. She understands love at its deepest levels and gives love from the highest unconditional place, which in my book makes her very special! People like Caroline not only help others to find the love in them, but also to help them see that love when it is given without condition has all the power, kindness and grace they will ever need to succeed in their mission. She is a sparkling jewel and I treasure her!

Andrew Hobbs
Poet and Channel for the Divine
Andrew-Hobbs.com

Caroline Palmy is one of my favorite authors in the spiritual community right now. Her openhearted sharing of her own experiences helps readers to understand that others have gone through the same thing as they have. Her mission is to help others grow, feel better about themselves, and connect not only with spirit, but more importantly, with themselves and with love.

Her peaceful, calming energy is contagious. She truly pulls people from their storms into her calm, loving environment when she works with them.

I'm lucky enough to call Caroline a friend, and I love seeing her work evolve and expand, spreading more light and love into the world.

Susan Ellis-Saller
Tarot Reader, Energy Healer, Business
Coach, Author, and Editor
SueEllisSaller.com

Caroline Palmy is a calm, wise voice and presence in this noisy and often confusing world. In her writing she shares her deep insights into her own personal expansion but moreover she takes the readers hand and offers guidance into living a life based on flow and love. It's powerful and moving. I'm so thankful that Caroline is sharing her voice and energy with the world!

Rachel Hansen
Intuitive Money Mindset Coach &
Inner-Work Guide.
Worthyaf.com

Being in Caroline's presence is calming and smoothing. She is a gentle soul with an abundance of loving kindness to share with everyone. Her books are healing, allowing each of us to pause and reflect; giving us permission to love ourselves a little more each day. Caroline has genuinely worked on her healing; on being and becoming. She's a courageous goddess who willingly shares the truth of her own story. Thank you for sharing yourself and your words with us Caroline, the world is so much the better for having you in it."

Rev. Deb Connor MBAcC
Author of *The Little Book of Dao* **&** *The 12 Step Colouring Book*, **Transformational Life Coach, Mixed Media Artist, Interfaith Minister & trainee Daoist Priest.**
DebConner.co.uk

ABOUT THE AUTHOR

Caroline Palmy is a Heart Flow Healer and award-winning author.

She helps gorgeous Empaths, Sensitive Souls, Earth Angels and Giving Hearts to come back into the flow of love.

Caroline cannot help but express and embody her heart and helps others to find express and embody their hearts, too.

She teaches from the heart, for the heart, and of the heart.

Her first book, *Conversations With Me*, was published July 2018 and won a mention on Janey Loves Platinum Award List.

You are holding Caroline's second book, *Loving Conversations With Me*, published in May 2019 in your hands.

Caroline lives in Switzerland, with her three (nearly) grown children, a golden retriever, a cat, and 9 tortoises. They are surrounded by nature.

She is finishing her memoir trilogy with the book, *Spiritual Conversations With Me*. Watch out for her next release.

She is also putting all her Wisdom Assignments—the Wisdom From Within from her first book and the Wisdom From the Heart from her second book into beautiful audio files, so that you can be lovingly guided through the amazing healing exercises.

If you like her writing, you can find many blog posts that cover the topics of self-love, healing, grief, and relationship healing on her website, PalmyHealing.com.

Guided meditations and beautiful, loving webinars in which she shares her insights and healing tools can be found in the Healing Shop on Caroline's website.

She also holds a loving space in her Open Hearted Sisterhood group on Facebook. Feel free to join her for daily insights into Self Love, Self Care, Celebrations and more.